How to B
Clinical Psychologist

Clinical psychology is a very popular and competitive career path for psychology students. This practical and accessible guide contains all the information and advice required by those considering pursuing a career in the field.

How to Become a Clinical Psychologist provides a clear overview of a career in clinical psychology, with chapters examining areas such as the educational and work experience requirements for selection, the doctoral training programmes and the personal qualities and attributes necessary for the profession. The training process is described and the wide range of career options post-qualification are outlined and supported with testimonials and first-hand accounts from clinical psychologists, current trainees and those aspiring to this career. Practical advice and examples are given throughout the guide, and a wide range of real-life examples bring the realities of this challenging yet rewarding career to life.

Written by established clinical psychologists who have extensive clinical experience in the NHS and in the selection and training of doctoral trainees, this book provides valuable information on the educational, vocational and personal requirements for the career.

The perfect guide for anyone interested in clinical psychology, *How to Become a Clinical Psychologist* is an indispensable resource for A-level students, undergraduates considering the discipline and anyone considering a career in this popular and fascinating profession.

Laura Golding is a Clinical Psychologist and Programme Director of the University of Liverpool's Doctorate in Clinical Psychology programme. Much of her career has been spent working in the NHS with adults with learning disabilities as well as training clinical psychologists.

Judith Moss works as a Consultant Clinical Psychologist in the NHS in Manchester's Community Adult Learning Disability Service. She is also a Senior Clinical Tutor on the Doctorate in Clinical Psychology training programme at the University of Manchester.

How to Become a Practitioner Psychologist

Series Editor: David Murphy

Psychology remains one of the most popular choices for an undergraduate degree, whilst an increasing number of postgraduate courses are directed either towards further academic study in a sub-discipline or a career in applied practice. But despite the growing numbers of people interested in a career in psychology, from A-level students to those looking for a career change, the various pathways to entry into the profession are not necessarily obvious.

The *How to Become a Practitioner Psychologist* series of books is aimed at providing a clear, accessible and reader-friendly guide to the routes available to becoming a practitioner psychologist. Providing both information and advice, including testimonials from those recently qualified, the series will include a title for each of the seven domains of psychology practice as regulated by the Health and Care Professions Council.

Each book in the series will provide an invaluable introduction to anyone considering a career in this fascinating profession.

David Murphy, FBPsS FRSA, is the 2019–20 President of the British Psychological Society (BPS). He is past chair of the BPS Professional Practice Board and former Director of the BPS Division of Clinical Psychology Professional Standards Unit. He has worked in the National Health Service for nearly 30 years, during which time he worked across many different medical specialties, led a clinical health psychology and neuropsychology service in a large acute hospital trust in London and went on to became Director of the Oxford Institute of Clinical Psychology Training.

How to Become a Clinical Psychologist
Laura Golding and Judith Moss

How to Become an Occupational Psychologist
Stephen Woods and Binna Kandola

How to Become an Educational Psychologist
Jeremy Swinson and Phil Stringer

How to Become a Sport and Exercise Psychologist
Martin Eubank and David Tod

How to Become a Counselling Psychologist
Elaine Kasket

www.routledgetextbooks.com/textbooks/howtopsy/

How to Become a Clinical Psychologist

Laura Golding and
Judith Moss

LONDON AND NEW YORK

First edition published 2019
by Routledge
2 Park Square, Milton Park, Abingdon, Oxon, OX14 4RN

and by Routledge
52 Vanderbilt Avenue, New York, NY 10017

Routledge is an imprint of the Taylor & Francis Group, an informa business

British Library Cataloguing-in-Publication Data
A catalogue record for this book is available from the British Library

Library of Congress Cataloging-in-Publication Data
Names: Golding, Laura, author. | Moss, Judith, 1969– author.
Title: How to become a clinical psychologist / Laura Golding and Judith Moss.
Description: Milton Park, Abingdon, Oxon ; New York, NY : Routledge, 2019. | Includes bibliographical references and index.
Identifiers: LCCN 2019004643 (print) | LCCN 2019006840 (ebook) | ISBN 9781315226859 (eBook) | ISBN 9780415786669 (hardback) | ISBN 9780415786676 (pbk.) | ISBN 9781315226859 (ebk)
Subjects: LCSH: Clinical psychology—Study and teaching.
Classification: LCC RC467 (ebook) | LCC RC467 .G65 2019 (print) | DDC 616.890076—dc23
LC record available at https://lccn.loc.gov/2019004643

ISBN: 978-0-415-78666-9 (hbk)
ISBN: 978-0-415-78667-6 (pbk)
ISBN: 978-1-315-22685-9 (ebk)

Typeset in Galliard
by Apex CoVantage, LLC

Visit the companion website: https://www.routledgetextbooks.com/textbooks/howtopsy/

Printed and bound in Great Britain by
TJ International Ltd, Padstow, Cornwall

Contents

Acknowledgements

This book arose largely from questions asked by people who are just beginning to find out about clinical psychology. The answers to their questions have been provided by many people who have generously shared their experiences and advice. We are grateful to everyone who gave up their precious time and talked with us, wrote to us, tolerated our questions and allowed us to quote them. Particular thanks go to the people who read and commented on early drafts; your support has helped to shape the content and ensure that a diverse range of voices are heard throughout the book. To talk with so many clinical psychologists has reminded us of the wealth of wisdom, kindness, curiosity and compassion to be found in the profession.

Many thanks to Andrew Bethell, Jan-Sher Bhatti, Gita Bhutani, Sarah Butchard, Rosie Cawley, Gemma Cherry, Jay Dudley, Sarah Dunstan, Marianne Durand, Louise Egan, Laura Gabbay, Jonah Gourlay, Kate Hellin, Jo Hemmingfield, Mariam Iqbal, Maleha Khan, Gundi Kiemle, Christy Laganis, James Lea, Anna Markman, Paul Markman, Nikki McClelland, Pádraig McDonnell, Kate McGrath, Emma Morris, Robin Muir, Craig Newnes, Suzanne Nightingale, Sarah Powell, Amanda Roberts, Christine Rogers, Agnesa Ruse, Ian Rushton, Linda Steen, Kate Strutt, Victoria Teggart, Cara Tobin, Helena Tucker, Abi Turner, Rachel Turner and students and staff from Xaverian College, Manchester the University of Liverpool Experts by Experience Group, the University of Manchester Community Liaison Group, the University of Liverpool's Doctorate in Clinical Psychology team and the University of Manchester's Doctorate in Clinical Psychology team.

We must also acknowledge and thank Alice Knight, author of the popular *How to Become a Clinical Psychologist: Getting a Foot in the Door*

(2002), for writing the first straightforward and accessible book on how to find out about and pursue this particular career.

Our thanks also go to David Murphy, Series Editor, who commissioned this book, for his guidance and comments on the draft chapters. We are similarly grateful to Russell George, Eleanor Reedy and Alexandra Butterworth at Routledge.

Introduction

David Murphy – Series Editor

Welcome!

Firstly, I would likely to welcome you to this book, which is one of a series of seven titles, each of which focuses on a different type of practitioner psychologist registered as a professional in the UK. One of the things that has always appealed to me about psychology is its incredible diversity; even within my own primary field of clinical psychology there is a huge range of client groups and ways of working. The books in this series are all written by practitioner psychologists who are not only experts in, but also hugely enthusiastic about, each of their areas of practice. This series presents a fascinating insight into the nature of each domain, the range of activities and approaches within it and also the fantastic variety there is across the different areas of practice. However, we have also made sure that we have answered the practical questions you may have, such as "*How long does it take to train?*", "*What do I need to do to get on a training course?*" and "*How secure will my income be at the end of it all?*" We very much hope that this book will be interesting and answer all your questions (even ones you didn't know you had!), and further information and resources are available on our series website (www.routledge.com/cw/howtobecomeapractitionerpsychologist).

Psychology as a profession

Psychology is still a relatively young profession compared to many long-established professions, such as law, medicine, accounting, etc.; however, it has grown incredibly rapidly over the last few decades. One of the first people to use the title "psychologist" in a professional context was an American named Lightner Witmer who, only just over a hundred years ago, established what is widely recognized as the world's first psychology clinic in Pennsylvania. Witmer came to study psychology after taking a degree in economics and postgraduate studies in political science and then working for a time as a school teacher. He went on to study experimental psychology at the University of Pennsylvania and then at a famous research laboratory in Leipzig, Germany. He subsequently became a pioneer in the application of experimental psychology ideas to the treatment of children with specific learning and speech difficulties.

At the beginning of the twentieth century, these early psychologists saw great possibilities in applying psychological concepts to help people achieve their potential. However, even they could scarcely imagine the scale and range of applications of psychology that would exist by the beginning of the twenty-first century. Psychologists now have well-established roles in schools, mental and physical health services, prisons, police and security services, multinational companies, sport training centres; essentially almost anywhere where there is a focus on understanding and changing human behaviour, which, of course, is pretty much everywhere!

This book, along with the other six titles in the series, is intended to provide people who are at the beginning of their careers, or those who are thinking about making a change, an insight into the different areas of professional psychology. We hope that you will not only gain an overview of the specific domain that psychology entails, but also a sense of what it is like to work as a practitioner on a day-to-day basis. We also aim to explain how to become qualified to practice in the area of professional psychology, right from school until being fully qualified. Furthermore, we hope to provide an idea of how careers in the different areas of psychology can develop over time and how the profession of psychology might change as it continues to develop in the future.

Studying psychology at school or college

One thing that many people love about psychology is just how broad it is. As an academic discipline it encompasses physiological workings of the brain and the nervous system, how we perceive sounds and language, how we make decisions and the treatment of mental health problems, to name just a few areas. In recent years psychology has become the second most popular first degree subject at UK universities; indeed, figures from the Higher Education Statistical Agency (HESA) show that a total of 80,000 students were studying, either full-time or part-time, for a first degree in psychology in the academic year 2016–17.

Psychology has become not only a popular A-level choice but also increasingly an option at GCSE level. It is therefore now possible to take the first step on a career journey in psychology at an early age, and, if you are considering A-levels or GCSE subjects, we would certainly encourage you to look at psychology options if they are offered at your school. However, it is by no means required to have studied psychology at either GCSE or A-level in order to follow a career in psychology. If psychology isn't offered at your school, or you opt to go for other subjects, this won't stop you going on to become a psychologist, if you decide that this is what you would like to do. On the other hand, contrary to some myths, psychology is considered a valid A-level choice for many other degrees apart from psychology; indeed, it is listed as a "preferred subject" by University College London in their general list of A-level subject choices (www.ucl.ac.uk/prospective-students/undergraduate/application/requirements/preferred-a-level-subjects).

The only GCSE subjects that are specifically required by UK universities to study psychology are maths and English. A-level psychology is usually listed as a "preferred" subject, but is currently not required by any UK university for entry to a psychology degree course, and there is no indication that this will change. Therefore, overall our advice would be that psychology is an interesting subject choice which can provide a good foundation for further study in psychology, or other subjects. However, psychology at A-level is by no means essential for a career as a psychologist, so we recommend basing the decision on what your strengths and interests are and also what subjects are required for any other degree options you want to keep open to you.

Routes into graduate psychology careers

The first compulsory step on the road to a psychology career is attaining ***Graduate Basis for Chartered Membership*** of the British Psychological Society, commonly known as GBC (in the past this was called Graduate

Basis for Registration, or GBR for short). You will see this referred to a number of times in this book and the other titles in the series. The British Psychological Society (BPS) is the professional body and learned society for psychology in the United Kingdom. It was established in 1901 to promote both academic and applied psychology and currently has over 60,000 members, making it one of the largest psychological societies in the world. There are two possible routes to attaining Graduate Basis for Chartered Membership of the British Psychological Society on the basis of UK qualifications.

A psychology undergraduate degree

The most common route is to complete an undergraduate degree in psychology that is accredited by the BPS; a lower 2nd-class degree classification or above is required for GBC. This doesn't need to be a single honours degree in psychology; it can be a joint degree with another subject. However, in order to be accredited it has to cover a core curriculum that is specified by the BPS and the provision must meet certain other standards. At the time of writing there are 578 BPS-accredited undergraduate courses offered at 126 different higher education institutions within the UK. Many of these courses are general psychology degrees however some focus more on specific domains, such as forensic psychology, health psychology, abnormal psychology, sport psychology, business psychology and so forth. About a third of all accredited undergraduate psychology undergraduate programmes involve combination with another subject, and the array of possible options is extensive, including business, English literature, education, maths, history, philosophy, physics, zoology and criminology, to name but a few. This range of choice could be a bit overwhelming, but it is important to bear in mind that virtually all psychology degrees do offer a significant choice of options within them, so two students doing the same generic psychology degree at the same institution may actually take quite a different mix of courses, albeit still with the same core psychology components. Moreover, it is also important to remember that even if the title of a degree appears very specific, the course will still cover the same core psychology content, if it is BPS-accredited.

For a career in professional psychology, the most important issue is attaining GBC; the subtle differences in the individual course content are far less important. Our advice would be to consider all the factors that are important to you about the choice of university and the psychology course, rather than getting too focused on the specific content of a course. You may wish to do a degree that allows you to specialise in an area of psychology that you are particularly interested in, and of course that's fine. However, in reality, all postgraduate professional training courses need to cater for people with a range of different psychology backgrounds, so whilst having done specialised options at undergraduate level might provide a good foundation to build on, it's very unlikely to mean you can jump ahead of those who didn't do those options at undergraduate level.

My own experience was that I did a joint degree with psychology and zoology. (I have to confess that I wasn't really sure what psychology was when I was choosing, so I hedged my bets!) Fairly early on I became interested in clinical psychology, but I still got a great deal out of studying other subjects that weren't anything to do with clinical psychology, including many of the zoology subjects. In my final year, I did an option in vertebrate palaeontology (better known as the study of dinosaurs!), mainly because it sounded interesting. In fact, it turned out to be one of the most stimulating and useful courses I have ever studied, and the lecturer was one of the best teachers I ever had. I learned how to interpret inconclusive evidence by using careful observation and deduction, rather than jumping to conclusions, and that generic skill has been very useful throughout my clinical psychology career. So my personal advice would be not to feel under any pressure to specialise in a particular branch of psychology too soon. I suggest you choose degree options because they are stimulating and well taught, *not* because you think they will look good on your CV. In reality, if you are applying for professional psychology training courses, what will stand out more on your CV will be really good grades, which come from being highly engaged and developing a thorough understanding of the areas you are studying.

Some psychology programmes offer a "professional placement year" within the degree. Such courses are often marketed on the basis that graduates have a higher employment rate on graduation; however, it is important to bear in mind that you will also be graduating a year later than people on a three-year course, and during the placement year most people will be receiving little or no pay and will still be paying fees (albeit at a reduced rate) to the university. My own personal opinion is that degrees with professional placements don't necessarily offer a significant advantage overall. On the one hand, if the course does have well-established placement opportunities, this can make it easier to get that first step on the ladder; however, there are many opportunities for getting postgraduate experience relevant to professional psychology, some of which are voluntary but many of which are paid.

Choosing a university to study psychology

As well as choosing a specific course, you will also need to choose individual universities to apply to. A detailed consideration of the different universities offering undergraduate psychology programmes is beyond the scope of this series, and there is a great deal of information freely available on the Web (starting with the University College Admissions Service (UCAS) website) and from schools and colleges. However, it is true to say that universities do vary somewhat, and, of course, the area in which they are located is also a factor to consider. The Unistats website (www.unistats.com) is the official website providing data gathered from the National Student Survey and other independent sources which can be used for comparing universities and individual courses. One particular issue that prospective applicants can be confused about is what is meant by a university being in the "Russell Group" and what the significance of this is. The Russell Group is a self-selected association of 24 research-intensive universities across the United Kingdom that was formed in 1994. Although they only account for 15% of all UK higher education institutions, Russell Group universities receive nearly 80% of all UK research funding. However, it does not necessarily follow that it is always better to do your psychology degree at a Russell Group university; indeed some of the most highly rated universities for psychology, such as the University of Bath and the University of St Andrews, were not members of the Russell Group at the time of writing. Whilst it is understandable to think that going for a well-known name or the Russell Group "brand-name" must be a safe bet, in order to find the best fit for *you*, there really is no alternative to doing a bit of research into individual universities and the specific course options they offer, and then going to visit to get the feel of the institution and the local area. After all, you will be investing three (or in some cases four) years of your life in this decision, so although it's certainly not something to stress out excessively about, it is worth putting a bit of time into.

University applications

Once you have chosen universities and specific courses you wish to apply for, you will need to apply via the University College Admissions Service (UCAS) website (www.ucas.com). The site contains a great deal of advice, and you should also access the advice available from your school or college. One of the things you will be required to do is to submit a personal statement (PS). The UCAS website has comprehensive general information about writing a personal statement, including a mind map and worksheet. The key principles of writing a PS are the same regardless of what course you are applying for, i.e. demonstrating you understand what the subject is about, conveying why you are interested in it and demonstrating that you have the skills required to successfully complete the course and make a positive contribution to the learning process. Providing evidence of things you have done which demonstrate your interest, enthusiasm and your abilities will inevitably carry more weight than simply saying "I am passionate about psychology". Furthermore, admissions tutors will also pay attention to how well-structured and well-written your personal statement itself is, since academic writing ability is important to success as a psychology undergraduate. If at this stage you are particularly interested in one career path within professional psychology then you will certainly want to mention this, although it would also be helpful to demonstrate that you understand what the career path involves and that an undergraduate degree is one step towards this. Sometimes people's own experience of mental health or emotional difficulties or that of a close friend or family member has influenced their interest in psychology and/or pursuing a career in psychology. Again, don't feel shy about mentioning this, although only if you feel comfortable doing so. However, don't lose sight of the purpose of the PS and what an admissions tutor will be looking for; lived experience can really help to understand the perspective of people with psychological, but you will need to cover the other skills required. Furthermore, since psychology is such a broad subject, it's important to bear in mind that you will need to study a whole range of topics, most of which will be unrelated to any one specific psychological problem. The Which? University website has a useful article about writing a PS for a psychology degree application (https://university.which.co.uk/advice/personal-statements/personal-statement-advice-psychology-students).

If you are studying for, or have completed, a psychology degree at a university outside of the UK, then your course will not have been accredited by the BPS. (At the time of writing, the BPS does accredit a small number of undergraduate programmes delivered outside the UK but these have to be awarded by a UK university). However, it is possible to apply for GBC on the basis of a psychology degree undertaken anywhere in the world, and the applications are assessed on an individual basis to establish whether the criteria are met (for further information, see the www.bps.org.uk/join-us/membership/graduate-membership).

Converting to psychology with a degree in a different subject

People who have done a first degree in something other than psychology (or those whose psychology degree did not meet the criteria for GBC) can still pursue a career in professional psychology; this route involves attaining GBC by doing a conversion course. At the time of writing, there were 78 BPS-accredited conversion courses in the UK. Most of these lead to an MSc, although some lead to a graduate diploma; most are quite general in their content and are titled simply "psychology" or "applied psychology", whereas others are more focused in specific areas like child development, mental health or even fashion. However, if they are BPS-accredited, all of these conversion courses will still cover the core psychology curriculum regardless of their title.

Since the core components are common between all BPS-accredited degree programmes, you certainly will not be committing yourself irrevocably to any one area of professional psychology through your choice of psychology undergraduate or postgraduate conversion course. In the clinical psychology programme that I run, we take people who have a range of different experiences at undergraduate level and some who did different first degrees altogether. Of course, when you come to postgraduate qualifications you do have to make more fundamental choices about the area of psychology you wish to focus on.

The different areas of psychology practice

The authors of each of the seven books in the series are, as you would expect, experts in, and very enthusiastic about, their own areas of psychology practice, and the rest of this book focuses pretty much exclusively on clinical psychology. Our aim across the series is to provide information about what each domain is about, what it is like to work in this area on a day-to-day basis and what the route to become qualified is like. What we have not done, and indeed could not do, is say which one of the domains is "best". The answer is that there is no one "best" type of psychologist; instead, we hope you will be able to find which area of practice seems to fit your own interests and strengths best. This can be difficult and we would encourage you to keep an open mind for as long as you can; you might be surprised to find that an area you hadn't really thought much about seems to be a good fit.

Once you have identified an area of practice that seems to fit you best, we would certainly recommend that you try and meet people who work in that area and talk to them personally. Even after you have embarked on postgraduate training in a particular field, don't feel it's too late to explore other areas. Indeed, there are areas of overlap between the different domains, so that psychologists with different training backgrounds might well end up working in a similar area. For instance, clinical and counselling psychologists often work together in psychological therapy services in the NHS, whereas health psychologists and occupational psychologists might work alongside each other in implementing employee health programmes.

My own journey in professional psychology started with my degree in psychology and zoology and led on to postgraduate training in clinical psychology and then working in the National Health Service. However, my journey also included going on to become registered as a health psychologist and a clinical neuropsychologist, and I went on to do management training and become a senior manager in the NHS before moving into clinical psychology training and then research in leadership development. Over the years, I have worked alongside colleagues from all of the domains at various times, particularly through roles with the British Psychological Society. I have been fascinated to learn even more about other domains through editing this series and, of course, as psychology is still such a young and dynamic field, new developments continue to emerge – you may become a Lightner Witmer for the twenty-first century, pioneering a new application of psychology that no-one has even thought of yet! I would therefore encourage you to think carefully about your career direction. However, whether your psychology "career" lasts just for the duration of this book, or for the rest of your working life, I would encourage you to maintain an open curious mind. In the words of one of my favourite sayings, "*It is better to travel well than to arrive*". We hope this book, and others in the series, will be of help to you wherever your own unique career journey takes you!

What does a clinical psychologist do?

As David Murphy, Series Editor, suggests in Chapter 1, there may be a number of reasons why you have chosen to pick this book up. Maybe you are a student considering which subjects to study at A-level, or equivalent, or wondering which career paths might be open to you if you were to study psychology? Perhaps you have already decided to study psychology at university and want to know more about possible career paths that might follow? You may have heard about clinical psychology and would like to know more about what this entails and how it differs from other sorts of psychology jobs? Or maybe you have already decided that clinical psychology looks like the career for you and you want to know as much about it as possible to ensure that you maximise your chances of success? Whatever your reason for choosing to read this particular book in this series, we hope that you find it useful and interesting.

Why did we decide to write this book?

There are several reasons that we are interested in letting people know about becoming a clinical psychologist. In our work, we come across lots of people who we think would make excellent clinical psychologists but who do not seem to know the best way forward. We also meet many others who are frustrated by how competitive it can be to secure a clinical psychology training place. We know others who have devoted a great deal of time and effort to pursuing clinical psychology as a career aspiration when they do not seem well suited to it, or are poorly informed about what it will entail. Our hope is that this book will help you to think about whether becoming a clinical psychologist is for you; whether you have the qualities and characteristics needed; and whether the job itself is something that you would find interesting and fulfilling. If you find that you have answered "yes" to those questions, then we hope to give you some straightforward information and advice about how best to proceed.

What is a clinical psychologist?

The British Psychological Society (BPS) defines psychology as "the scientific study of the mind and how it dictates and influences our behaviour, from communication and memory to thought and emotion" (www.bps.org.uk/public/what-is-psychology). As a discipline, the aim of clinical psychology is to reduce psychological distress and enhance the promotion of psychological well-being.

> Clinical psychologists provide face-to-face therapy for individuals, families and groups. They also supervise and teach other professions to provide psychological treatments. Clinical psychologists apply the science of psychology to a range of clinical health care services. Clinical psychologists use this knowledge to design, implement and evaluate health care services that enhance well-being and minimise ill health and impairment. They are trained to apply their knowledge in systematic methods and practice which are scientifically evaluated and to test clinical practice for its effectiveness. Clinical psychologists offer leadership in organisational development, audit, service redesign and development.
>
> British Psychological Society, 2014

How do you become a clinical psychologist?

We have been asked this question hundreds of times throughout our working lives and throughout the rest of the book we hope to provide the best answers we can. We must, however, acknowledge that the context of the National Health Service (NHS) and UK clinical psychology training changes rapidly and that advice can become out of date very quickly. As it went to print, this book was up to date regarding the current arrangements for funding clinical psychology training (details of which can be found in Chapters 4 and 5), but it is important for you to check before you apply to see if changes have occurred over time.

How do we know what we are talking about?

We have each learned a great deal from our own roles in the profession, but, more importantly, our jobs mean that we have been able to talk with many other people who have tried (and sometimes failed) to become clinical psychologists, including trainee clinical psychologists and a range of qualified clinical psychologists at different stages in their careers. By seeking their opinions and sharing their experiences, we feel that we can give a broad view of the profession and the diverse range of work within it. We have also talked with many other people who have important opinions about clinical psychology, including people who have worked with clinical psychologists as patients, clients and colleagues.

Who are we?

Laura has worked for two of the UK's doctorate in clinical psychology programmes (Lancaster University and the University of Liverpool), as well as working for 16 years in NHS clinical services, and Jude has worked for the University of Manchester's Doctorate in Clinical Psychology programme for 17 years and in the NHS for 28 years.

Laura's story

I became interested in psychology when studying for my A-levels. I read a book on perception which I found fascinating and decided that psychology was definitely the subject of further study for me. I went on to do a Bachelor of Arts (BA) in psychology at the University of Manchester. At that stage, I had no idea what I wanted to do after university, but I loved studying psychology. In the third year I chose a specialist module on working with people with learning disabilities, older adults and people with long-term mental health difficulties. It was largely taught by clinical psychologists working in the NHS. Hearing the lecturers talk about their work and how they applied their knowledge of psychology intrigued and inspired me. I asked one of the guest lecturers, "How can I become a clinical psychologist?" He managed a large NHS clinical psychology service and invited me to work as a volunteer in his service after I graduated. I spent that summer in what was then called a long-stay mental health hospital, collecting research data, observing clinical sessions and generally doing whatever I could do to be helpful. I subsequently got a job as a support worker in a day centre for young adults with learning disabilities in Manchester. In this job I learned much about working with people with a range of disabilities and about how to support people who often felt distressed and misunderstood and whose behaviour was, at times, distressing to others, including me.

A year later I got a job as an assistant psychologist in an NHS service in East London. Much of the job involved resettling adults with learning disabilities from a long-stay hospital into the community. That year, I applied to do clinical psychology training and secured a place on what was then an in-service course in Lancashire (which is now the programme at Lancaster University). My clinical training was hard work, but I enjoyed the whole experience and working with a diverse range of service user groups in a variety of work settings. After my training, I worked in adult primary care and in a learning disabilities service. Eighteen months later, I took a part-time post as a clinical tutor for a clinical psychology training programme. I loved working with people with learning disabilities, their families and paid staff. I liked thinking on my feet, working with uncertainty and the many different ways of working. Throughout my career to date, my clinical work has remained in services for people with learning disabilities whilst also doing a range of other jobs in training. For the past nine years I have worked for the Doctorate in Clinical Psychology training programme at the University of Liverpool, where I am the programme director. I have supervised numerous trainees on their learning disabilities' placements and have done many visits to trainees on placements. I have guided many trainees through their clinical training and am involved in the selection processes for the programme. My work as a clinical psychologist is rarely boring, can be stressful and, at times, frustrating because of the wider service, societal and political context. Clinical psychologists can help people to make positive changes in their lives. We can often be advocates where there are inequalities and injustices, and we have the skills and knowledge to listen and to be alongside those in distress. I always remind myself that clinical psychologists are first and foremost human beings and we have the capacity, and power, to do harm as well as good. Knowing this, from the outset, when considering this career choice is important.

Jude's story

After my O-levels (GCSE equivalent), I studied psychology, sociology and English at college, where the combination of good teaching and interesting curriculum meant it was easy to decide to study psychology at university. Once there, returning from lectures and hearing about the subjects my flatmates were studying, I remember thinking that my day had been so much more interesting than theirs and seemed to have many more practical applications. I enjoyed the fact that in a single day I might be dissecting a brain in one workshop, thinking about models of memory in the next lecture, meeting someone with a diagnosis of dissociative identity disorder in a seminar and then looking at research on moral development in children. No two days were the same, which has characterised my career ever since.

It was at university that I decided to pursue clinical psychology as a career. Voluntary work with people who had experienced head injury had sparked my interest in how the body and mind interact and I had considered studying medicine, but what I learned about mental health and what was then called "abnormal psychology", was much more intriguing. On leaving university, I worked as an assistant psychologist in a long-stay hospital for people with learning disabilities and my eyes were opened to some of the social and political aspects of the work that made me realise how powerful an impact psychologists can have – both positive and otherwise.

After training at the University of Manchester I began working in the NHS, initially in adult primary care mental health (primary care) and a service for people with learning disabilities. After a while I gave up the former and have been working as a clinician in learning disability services ever since, more recently in a managerial role. I have found the clinical work to be fascinating and it has been a joy and privilege to work with the individuals and families I have met over the years. The job has also taught me a great deal about the importance of patience, humour and kindness as well as academic rigour.

Over the years I have worked with many clinical psychologists, recruited and interviewed many times and talked with enough clients and families to have developed a sense of what qualities are important in clinical psychologists to whom one could turn in times of distress: wisdom, humanity, openness to difference, knowledge, skills and professionalism.

Since 2002, I have also worked on the doctoral training programme in clinical psychology at the University of Manchester. As a senior clinical tutor I have been involved in the selection of trainees and have been responsible for supporting many trainees throughout their training. Much of my work involves helping trainees to develop the professional and personal competencies that will enable them to become valued clinicians who enjoy their work and practice with strong ethical principles underpinning respectful and effective practice. It is a source of great pride to play a part in people becoming the kind of clinician who I would feel comfortable to see or would recommend to anyone who needed support.

In recent years, Laura and I have developed links with a local sixth form college and meet with A-level psychology students who are applying to university to study psychology as an undergraduate degree. It is their questions and concerns that have largely guided the content of this book.

A quick note on language and labels

If you are interested in psychology you will probably have noticed that there are lots of terms and labels used to describe different people and human experience, and it can be really confusing to know which words are acceptable to use. The language we use to describe ourselves and others, to talk about what has happened to us or to convey how people feel and behave, is powerful and important. There has been a great deal written about this that is beyond the scope of this book to review, but we want to say a few words about it before we begin.

We know that language and the choice of words that we use convey meaning. For example, think about how differently you might feel to be described as a patient or a client or a service user, which are all very common terms in the NHS. Each has a different meaning and says something about your position, power and choice. Likewise, there are strong views about language used about mental health: consider, for example, how different it might feel to be described as "a schizophrenic", or as "someone who has a diagnosis of schizophrenia" or as someone who feels distressed and preoccupied by hearing voices that other people don't hear. As another example, think about the meaning conveyed by saying that someone has "committed suicide" with its connotations of a criminal act, as opposed to someone having "ended their own life" or "killed themselves". It is important to be mindful about the effects of labels and to ensure that people have choice about how they are described. We must also be conscious that, because of the ways in which mental health, psychological distress and different "ways of being" are viewed in our society, even language that started life as "neutral" can become imbued with meaning and become unacceptable. Consider how the once acceptable terms "mentally subnormal", "retarded" and "imbecile" would now be viewed and how the development of the label of "mental handicap" was replaced with "learning disability" and more recently "intellectual disability".

We raise this subject here, early in the book, to acknowledge that the language we use to talk about people and their lives really does matter. It speaks of attributions about cause and beliefs about the future. It indicates our conscious and less conscious views and judgements, about the value of different people and their experience. There are so many different views on this that it can be easy to feel overwhelmed and paralysed by the desire "not to get it wrong". Our view is that remaining respectful and careful makes serious errors less likely and a certain degree of clumsiness is to be forgiven in us all. It is also hard to go far wrong if we ensure that we hold in mind how individuals and groups wish to be described.

Throughout this book, we have tended to use the language that is most commonly used by clinical psychologists in practice today and which the Experts by Experience (EbEs) with whom we work have said that they prefer. Many clinicians who work in parts of the NHS closely related to medical practice refer to the people they support as "patients"; others use the term "clients" or "service users" where they wish to avoid the intimation of illness or a medical model. You will see all of these words in this book. When people who have used psychological services or worked in therapy with a clinical psychologist are involved in the development or review of services, or use their experience and learning to share with us, they may be referred to as consultants, Experts by Experience, service users or patient representatives, depending on the context.

Them and us?

One of the hardest balances to strike is to recognise that when we use labels to describe a certain group of people – for example, people with learning disabilities or people who have experienced depression – there is an implicit assumption that they are *other* people. The terms "patient", "client" and "service user" all imply people who are *not us*. Labels have power and utility for good and bad, but it is crucial that we do not fall into this trap of "us and them" thinking. We clinical psychologists are also people who are impacted by our experiences, by our psychobiology, and, like everyone else, we experience severe psychological and emotional distress that is sometimes described as mental illness. We must recognise that there is no them and us – we are all human and vulnerable to experiences that reduce our well-being. Recent research suggests that the level of psychological distress and mental health problems for clinical psychologists is high, as it is in other areas of the medical and helping professions ("Honest, open & proud"; Rhodes, 2017). This level of distress may be partly a result of a working life that is suffused with the experience of being with people in distress, but it might also bring the opportunity to become "experts with experience" who have the capacity to empathise with the people with whom we work. A recently qualified clinical psychologist sums this up well and describes how this can be beneficial in working with service users:

> *The experience of using mental health services can be your biggest asset. But, only if you learn to use your experiences to collaborate,*

to minimise the power differential between you and your clients, to empower, to enable human rights and to emotionally connect with a client's distress. Empathy is preferable to sympathy.

Who else will you hear from in this book?

To help us describe what it is like to work as a clinical psychologist, to apply for training and to be a trainee (and much more), we have talked to a large number of people to find out about their experiences, opinions and advice for people who are considering following the same route. We aim to give a flavour of the range of roles clinical psychologists play and also to include a range of different perspectives on this career choice. According to the British Psychological Society (BPS), 95% of clinical psychologists work in the NHS, so we have tried to ensure that the voices you will hear reflect that, but we also want you to hear from clinical psychologists who have taken career paths outside the NHS. To help us ensure that we are representing views from across the profession and beyond, we have talked with:

- A-level students at sixth form colleges
- Current undergraduates studying psychology
- People who have worked with clinical psychologists as patients/clients and then as colleagues
- Trainee clinical psychologists from two university doctorate in clinical psychology programmes
- Recently qualified clinical psychologists, including those working in the NHS, at universities and overseas
- Senior clinical psychologists working in the NHS, university and private practice in the UK and overseas.

Facts and figures

Clinical psychology is a relatively small profession, but the variety of work it involves is wide. In September 2018, there were 23,404 practitioner psychologists registered with the Health and Care Professions Council (HCPC). The last recorded figures indicate that there are over

8000 clinical psychologists working in the NHS (BPS, 2011) and there will also be many working privately. These clinicians work in a wide variety of settings doing a range of diverse and fascinating jobs, and the way that one clinical psychologist spends their working life may look nothing like another who has the same job title.

In the UK in 2018, 593 people started their training to become clinical psychologists on the 30 UK university training programmes, for whom applications are administered by the Clearing House for Postgraduate Courses in Clinical Psychology (www.leeds.ac.uk/chpccp/). A total of 3866 people applied to train through the Clearing House – 15% were successful in gaining a place for clinical training. We will tell you more about how to apply for clinical psychology training in Chapter 4 and about what clinical psychology training involves in Chapter 5.

Essential personal characteristics

Before we start describing in detail what clinical psychology is (and is not) and how to apply for training, it is crucial to consider whether you have the personal characteristics needed to become a good clinical psychologist. We raise this from the outset as we believe that there are certain characteristics that are essential to becoming a good clinical psychologist and if you do not have them then this may not be the career path for you. The personal attributes and characteristics described below are largely determined by the opinions of Experts by Experience (EbEs) – that is, people who are or have been recipients of the services of clinical psychologists and/or wider mental health services, or carers.

This list includes items taken from work carried out by the Community Liaison Group, the EbE group of the University of Manchester's Doctorate in Clinical Psychology training programme which are consistent with similar work taken by other EbE groups working in collaboration with clinical psychology training programmes elsewhere in the UK.

Are the following attributes and qualities ones that you can demonstrate?

Genuine respectful curiosity about people. Each person will have a unique life history and it is important to respond with a non-judgemental attitude that demonstrates a genuine desire to help in a way that is meaningful to the individual. EbEs note the central importance of balance, equality and mutual respect within the therapeutic relationship.

Kindness and the capacity for empathy, demonstrating a desire to understand how someone is feeling and how life is from their perspective. EbEs note that people do not expect a therapist to "have all the answers" and have often had experiences where "being told what to do" was experienced as unhelpful. Humility, ordinariness, realism, honesty and recognition of one's own limitations will foster the foundations of a truly collaborative relationship.

The capacity for hard work and resilience. Clinical psychologists need to demonstrate the willingness to be alongside people who may be very different from themselves and who may be extremely distressed. Often the work takes place in challenging organisations and to be able to work successfully as a clinical psychologist you need to have stamina and personal resilience.

The willingness to gain and share knowledge. People value being helped by experts in evidence-based approaches, and collaboration is most effective when professionals also value and respect that service users are also "Experts by Experience", enabling a process of sharing of knowledge to take place.

Finally, one of our EbE colleagues sums up key skills by emphasising the importance of listening well – "*Make certain that you are listening to what people are telling you, not just listening to what you want to hear. If you do this you can make an enormous difference to the quality of many people's lives*".

What do clinical psychologists do?

In this part of the chapter, we tell you about being a clinical psychologist and answer the questions people regularly ask us when considering studying psychology or becoming a clinical psychologist. These questions include:

- What do clinical psychologists actually do?
- Who do they work with?
- What sort of organisations do clinical psychologists work in?
- What is clinical psychology *not*?

- What are the differences between clinical psychology and psychiatry, psychotherapy and counselling?
- How much are clinical psychologists paid?
- What are the best and worst things about the work that clinical psychologists do?

What does a clinical psychologist actually do?

This is a much harder question to answer than you might imagine because clinical psychologists do such a wide variety of tasks; one person's job may look completely unlike that of someone else. Perhaps the best way of answering is to note that there are roles that most clinical psychologists play to a greater or lesser extent in their working lives. We will examine these in more detail after an overview and introduction to what clinical psychologists do.

The work of clinical psychology

Clinical psychologists are primarily involved in working with people to reduce psychological distress and improve psychological well-being and functioning. However, this is more complex than simply saying "diagnosis A leads to the delivery of treatment B"; to determine what the most effective and relevant interventions might be requires a good understanding of a problem. For this reason, clinical psychologists are interested in *why* a situation or problem exists. Rather than jumping to conclusions about what is wrong, a clinical psychologist will try to generate a range of different ideas about why a situation or a problem has come about in the context of a person's life, and then, together with the client or patient, look at further evidence to either prove or disprove those ideas and determine the best form of intervention. Our best guesses (or hypotheses) are based on evidence from what the psychological literature tells us and what we can learn about someone by the assessments we do. That is why research is so important to psychologists. For this career it helps, therefore, to be curious about others and about life and to be comfortable with "not knowing" and "finding out".

Clinical psychologists use psychological theories to try and understand the difficulties that individuals or families are having and to come up with ways of helping. As we work with such a variety of people experiencing a wide range of problems, we must be able to draw on a large evidence base and ensure we are as open-minded as possible. One of the best ways to do this is to make sure we collaborate with patients and clients. Experts by Experience are central in determining that the developing research is asking the right questions in the right way, and properly sharing the emerging knowledge in the most useful and effective ways.

Usually the first step is to work out what a problem is, and although this might sound obvious, often it is not. Clinical psychologists try to avoid using simplistic diagnostic labels that can lead to simplistic treatment (for example, "this person has schizophrenia therefore they need to take this drug"), instead aiming to understand each individual's experience. So, for example, if someone is struggling with low mood – which means they feel hopeless about themselves and the future – this is clearly a problem for them and their quality of life, but the problem might also include difficulties in their relationships, their housing or finances, not being able to work, drinking too much and changes in their physical well-being. Someone else who might also be given a diagnosis of depression may be having an entirely different experience and set of difficulties which affects their life in different ways. Primarily, though, clinical psychologists focus on who an individual is, their difficulties and capabilities, and what has happened to them. Developing this individual understanding of this is a process we call formulation, and it is a central aspect of the role of clinical psychology. We will say more about formulation later.

It is often the case that the person who is referred to a clinical psychologist is not the person who has "the problem". A child who has begun to have "tantrums" is unlikely to see this behaviour as a problem, whereas his or her parents might have a different view. Someone who does not fully understand risk might open themselves up to exploitation without seeing this as problematic in the way that their support staff do. So clinical psychologists begin their assessments by finding out what the problem is and for whom it is a problem. Often this is not clear-cut and there are a number of very different perspectives. Usually, at this stage, the clinical psychologist will have some ideas (or hypotheses) about what is going on. For example, if they have been asked to see an older person who has become confused and seems to be hearing things that other people cannot hear, they might be asking themselves questions about whether that person's mood is low, whether they are recalling past traumatic experiences, whether they may be in the early stages of dementia or if they might have a urinary tract infection. We know from clinical practice and research that all those factors could lead to a person experiencing such problems.

The next step is for the clinical psychologist to undertake an assessment to find out more about the problem and to look at the evidence to support or disprove their hypotheses – or come up with some other best guesses. Assessments might include:

- Meeting with and interviewing the individual and, with their consent, other people who might have a view about what is happening, such as family members, teachers or support or nursing staff.
- Obtaining more information from other professionals, such as medical tests, previous diagnoses and background history.
- Using standardised measures of cognitive functioning.
- Using a standardised measure of mood or other psychological factors.
- Observation of the person's behaviour.
- Recording of behaviour, mood and other areas of concern.

Once all of the information is gathered and combined, the clinical psychologist and their client/patient can work together to figure out which are the most troubling difficulties and what aspects of the formulation are most helpful in deciding options for making change. The clinical psychologist can discuss what the person wants to be different, the range of intervention approaches and the pros and cons of each to allow the client to decide how they want to proceed. They will decide with the person what change and outcomes are important and how to measure whether any change has occurred.

Roles that clinical psychologists undertake

The preceding description gives an introduction to the work that a clinical psychologist might do and shows some of the range of roles that most clinical psychologists play to a greater or lesser extent in their work. These are described further in the following sections.

Psychological assessment

The first stage of almost all aspects of a clinical psychologist's work is to do some "finding out", which involves gathering information about the person, people or situation that they are concerned with. This almost always involves interviewing clients and other relevant parties, but may also include using psychometric tests (which are standardised assessments that aim to objectively measure aspects of an individual's mental or intellectual ability, personality, brain function or behaviour), using questionnaires and measures of mood, designing individual measures and records of thoughts and behaviours, using observational methods for looking at behaviour or using interview techniques for talking to individuals and groups.

Psychological formulation: This is a core aspect of clinical psychology and it is a word you will hear over and over again. Formulation means trying to make sense of why something is the way it is – working out how someone's life experiences, genetics, profile of cognitive and neurological abilities, family history, beliefs, relationships, social context and many other factors have led them to be who they are in their current situation and what keeps things that way. It is a shared understanding and a way of making sense of difficulties; it provides "best guesses" (hypotheses), based on the evidence available, about what is going on for a person or a family. You can find out more about psychological formulation by having a look at a book written by Johnstone and Dallos (2013) and more about the sorts of work that clinical psychologists do in a book edited by Davey, Lake and Whittington (2015). In addition, the Power Threat Meaning Framework (British Psychological Society, Division of Clinical Psychology, 2018) brings together a psychological approach aimed at helping to identify and understand patterns of emotional distress, unusual experiences and troubled or troubling behaviour.

Interventions using a range of different models of therapy: Clinical psychologists are trained in a number of models of psychological therapy which they undertake with individuals or with couples or groups. There are many different sorts of psychological therapies and interventions, and it is beyond the scope of this book to describe them in detail, but there are several books that provide useful introductory overviews (e.g. Weatherhead and Flaherty-Jones, 2011) and the British Psychological Society's (BPS) website can be helpful as well as the NHS's "Moodzone", which gives brief introductions to different therapies (www.nhs.uk/conditions/stress-anxiety-depression/types-of-therapy/).

Research: Clinical psychologists are trained to carry out research at doctoral level. By carrying out high quality research we can answer important questions about what kinds of conditions and experiences lead some people to develop certain difficulties; what protects other people from psychological distress; what sorts of approaches and interventions work best for what sorts of people and when psychological approaches should be used instead of or in combination with other treatment approaches. The research itself is important, but it is also crucial for clinicians to be able to read, summarise and critique research done by others and to use that evidence-based knowledge in their clinical practice.

Service development: The development of knowledge about how best to support people is of little value unless it actually leads to people receiving better support. Developing services to deliver the most effective psychological interventions in the most efficient ways is part of the work of many clinical psychologists.

Audit: Once research has established the standards of best practice in psychological work, it is important that we check how well we are performing against those standards. This process of audit is an important aspect of clinical psychology work. Most clinical psychologists work in the NHS, which is publicly funded, and all psychologists tend to work with people in distress who are vulnerable. It is crucial, therefore, that we check that the work we do is of the highest quality and meets all the standards of safety and quality. Undertaking audit work is a part of what enables us to do this.

Teaching and training: Many clinical psychologists have roles in the teaching and training of others – either junior members of the profession, colleagues in other professions or unqualified support staff. For example, clinical psychologists are routinely involved in the training of medical staff and people from other health care professions, and often contribute to the training of police, probation, social care staff and people working in education.

Supervising the work of other clinical psychologists or other professionals: Providing supervision of clinical practice is an important role for many clinical psychologists and is key to ensuring safe practice. Clinical psychology is a small profession and yet the psychological literature is large and has applications to almost all elements of human life and certainly all aspects of health care. Many other professional jobs have important aspects of psychology to them, so supervision and consultation about how psychological knowledge can most effectively impact on the work of others is an important part of the role.

Consultation: Clinical psychologists are often asked to give advice and guidance to other people. Many professions require psychological skills and knowledge. Arguably, the best doctors, police and teachers are those people who are able to think about what the individuals with whom they interact need, how best to communicate to get good outcomes and how to respond when people do not do what they want or think is best. They will often seek advice from clinical psychologists about particular sorts of psychological difficulty or how best to approach a problem – examples include how to work with people who have a diagnosis of autism; how to adapt their methods for people who have a diagnosis of personality disorder; how best to manage self-harm in schools; how to support children after trauma or how best to look after the well-being of other professions in helping roles.

You can find out more in a book edited by Llewelyn and Murphy (2014). It is also important to remember that there are different perspectives on clinical psychology as a profession, including some critiques – see, for example, Newnes (2014).

How is clinical psychology different from other jobs?

There are a whole range of psychological professions; six other applied psychology careers are described in the other books in this series. Whereas some of these professions will have significant overlap with clinical psychology, others share very little except that they also draw on the psychological evidence base. It can be confusing and difficult to work out how these jobs differ, so we will give you a brief explanation of two of the most common ones.

How are clinical psychologists different from psychiatrists?

The professions of psychiatry and clinical psychology are both interested in mental health and well-being and offer assessments and a wide range of treatments to people experiencing psychological and emotional distress, and as such there is some overlap in their work. Psychiatrists are medically trained doctors who, after a general medical training, choose to specialise in mental health. Psychologists train in psychology from the start and are not medically trained. Important differences include that, in the UK, psychiatrists are able to prescribe medication and clinical psychologists are not. Psychiatrists often have roles under the Mental Health Act and most clinical psychologists do not, unless they choose to undertake further specific training.

Although there are a range of different routes into the profession, on average it takes about eight to ten years to train to be a clinical psychologist (three or four years undergraduate study, an average of two to three year of work experience and three years to complete doctoral level qualification). Psychiatrists undertake five years of undergraduate medical training followed by two years of foundation posts before specialist psychiatry training – which often takes another three years as a core trainee and four years as a specialist trainee to complete. In terms of working conditions, like clinical psychologists, psychiatrists work in a range of different clinical settings, both in hospitals and the community. Their salary scales mean they often earn more than clinical psychologists but may be working on-call shift-based rotas, which is still relatively unusual for a clinical psychologist.

As you can imagine, there can be a somewhat different approach to psychological distress depending on whether or not you adopt the primary approach of a medical model. This is the idea that mental illness is like physical illness – there is some underlying disorder which is diagnosed by assessing symptoms of thoughts, feelings and behaviours that occur together in patterns and are treated with medication and other physical approaches. The alternative psychological model states that although genetics, biology, neurology and neurochemistry are often crucial to the development of a difficulty, psychological distress is not a foregone conclusion. Instead, psychological distress is understood as the result of emotional and psychological experiences, the social and relational contexts in which these occur and how an individual responds. Generally speaking, clinical psychologists are more likely to ask the question, "What has happened to you?" than "What is wrong with you?" It is easy to characterise psychiatry and clinical psychology as having directly opposing views but, in truth, there are a wide range of views and opinions across both professions. Most clinical psychologists and psychiatrists recognise that people are a complex interaction of their biology (their genetics, their brains and bodies), their psychology (thinking, perception and emotion), and what has happened to them (relationships, environments and experiences). The exact ways that all of these factors come together to make an individual and the way they experience their life is unknown, but psychiatry and psychology contribute to the deepening understanding and consequent development of approaches that can help those who are distressed.

How are clinical psychologists different from counselling psychologists?

Again, there are probably more similarities than differences between these two professions. Counselling psychology emerged from the practice of humanistic counselling, and much more detail can be found in the book in this series that specifically focuses on this. Gaining a training place in counselling psychology is a competitive process, although perhaps to a lesser extent than clinical psychology. Unlike clinical psychology, trainee counselling psychologists are not NHS employees; they are self-funded and have to find their own training placements, which can make it more challenging to gain experience with a range of client groups.

Counselling psychologists are required to gain a certain number of hours of supervised practice and be able to deliver a number of different models of therapy, whereas clinical psychologists are assessed using a competence-based framework that does not require a particular number of hours of supervised practice. Clinical psychology training programmes have to prove that they train clinicians to be competent in two or more therapeutic approaches, one of which must be cognitive behaviour therapy (CBT). In terms of the content of training, one of the notable differences is that clinical psychology retains a focus on neuropsychology and the value of psychometric assessment in contributing to formulations for some people, although this has started to become more common in counselling psychology.

To find out more about counselling psychology, we recommend that you read the relevant book in this series and look at the information on the BPS website (https://careers.bps.org.uk/area/counselling). There are also useful discussion threads on clinpsy.org.uk.

The amount of overlap between the psychological and psychotherapeutic helping professions can make it really difficult to work out which might suit you best and the implications of each career choice in terms of training costs and time, likely employment after training and the experience you will have. The other books in this series, the websites and resources we have noted, will help to give you a flavour of what might suit you best.

Who do clinical psychologists work with?

Clinical psychologists work with a very wide range of people. Anyone can experience psychological distress, no matter what their age, gender, religious or cultural background or life experience. We know that, in our society, about a quarter of us will experience a significant mental health problem at some time in our lives and all of us have fluctuations in our emotional and psychological well-being throughout our lives. The long history of research in psychology and psychiatry, together with the related fields of sociology, medicine and anthropology, have helped us to learn a great deal about the factors that make some people more vulnerable to significant levels of distress than others and to develop approaches that can help, particularly in relation to prejudice, inequality and disadvantage.

It is common in the UK for psychological services to be organised around the particular group of people who will be using them. We describe these services here using examples of clinical psychologists describing their work, including some typical "days in the life of".

Adult mental health: This generally refers to adults of working age, i.e. 18 to 65 years and includes:

Primary care: Primary care refers to services provided at the "first point of contact" – usually the General Practitioner (GP). Historically, primary care services work with people experiencing common mental health problems, usually labelled as depression, anxiety disorders, eating disorders and post-traumatic stress disorder (PTSD). This is not to imply that the distress experienced is not serious – in fact it can have a huge impact on the quality of someone's life and can be life threatening. The complexity of work undertaken by clinical psychologists in primary care has increased enormously over recent years.

The IAPT (Improving Access to Psychological Therapies) programme was established in 2008 in order to provide quicker access to a range of psychological interventions (initially this was primarily CBT, though the range of therapeutic approaches offered has increased). As a result, a large workforce of psychological practitioners, providing some of the less complex interventions to large numbers of people, have joined clinical psychologists working in primary care.

A day in the life of a clinical psychologist working in a primary care psychological therapy service

I tend to work an 8 am to 4 pm working day, as many clients prefer appointments outside normal working hours, so often my first clinical appointment is at 8 am. I get to work a little while before my first client so I can review my notes.

7.45 am: Arrive at work and turn on computer.
8.00 am: First patient – Sheila, who presents with long-standing issues with depression, linked to earlier life trauma. I am using a meta-cognitive approach to help her tackle this.
9.00 am: Second patient – Kevin, who was referred with complex interpersonal difficulties, including social anxiety, and anger-related issues. At the moment we are using a compassionate mind approach together.
10.00 am: Case admin for Sheila and Kevin, which includes writing notes and scoring of clinical measures.
10.40 am: Discuss a difficult clinical issue about consent to treatment for someone who is very unwell and, therefore, might not be able to give fully informed consent with a colleague who sits next to me in our shared office space.

11.00 am: Supervision session. I provide clinical supervision to one of our junior clinicians on a weekly basis. We discuss two of her cases in some depth today.

12.00 pm: We have a nice sandwich shop nearby, so I nip out to buy something to eat. I will bring that back and sit at the computer today, because I have to make some calls to colleagues in secondary care services relating to a couple of my clients who are presenting with risk issues. I also make a call to a social worker regarding another patient and some concerns around safeguarding.

1.00 pm: New patient, Mary, who I saw a couple of years ago. She is coming back to the service because her low mood has returned; it's linked to her history of childhood abuse, and appears to have been triggered again by difficulties in her relationship. Previously she derived some benefit from a broadly cognitive behavioural approach to help her symptoms, with a more integrative formulation of her overall experience.

2.00 pm: Another client session – Emily – who was referred with "Emotionally Unstable Personality Disorder". I have only seen her once before, so we are still building our assessment and formulation. A schema-based approach to help her understand and manage her difficulties feels like it will be very suitable.

3.00 pm: Time to write up notes for Mary and Emily, and I need to write an initial report to Mary's GP to let her know that Mary is now being seen.

3.50 pm: I am keen not to fall too far behind with internal communications, so I spend some time checking emails and ensuring anything of particular importance is read. I note others for when I have more time – possibly if I get a cancellation or non-attendance.

4.15 pm: I keep a list of issues pending from today, including needing to chase up the social worker re that safeguarding issue, as she wasn't available. Note to self to ensure patient notes are complete following that telephone call.

Secondary care: This generally refers to services for people experiencing what are deemed to be more severe and enduring mental health problems, such as psychosis, serious personality disorders and life-threatening eating disorders. Patients in secondary care services can also be those for whom a primary care intervention has not been beneficial. There are often clinical psychologists in Community Mental Health Teams (CMHTs) that support people to live at home and specialist teams that work with people experiencing their first episode of psychosis. Other clinical psychologists work with people for whom hospital-based treatment is required.

Children and adolescents: Clinical psychologists work with individual children and adolescents using a specialist range of therapeutic approaches, but they also work with parents, families and schools and with children who live in care.

A day in the life of a clinical psychologist working with children and young people

I always like to get in early to work, to clear a few emails and plan for anything outside of my diary commitments, such as reports and longer-term pieces of work that I'm chipping away at. The day officially starts with clinical supervision of a nursing colleague who works in the paediatric liaison part of our team, which I oversee and contribute to. We consider some cases that she is feeling stuck with and discuss re-emerging challenges that she is facing across her caseload; namely knowing when to end therapy. As clinical lead for the service I'm then off to a commissioner-led meeting about improving children's services. There are lots of agencies present, so the agenda isn't entirely about CAMHS (Child and Adolescent Mental Health), but as "mental health is everyone's business" I try to ensure consideration is given to well-being at all available junctures, including coffee breaks when some of the best opportunities to influence arise. I'm back to base to have a meeting with managers about our throughput of cases, making sure that despite the pressure to reduce waiting times we still deliver effective therapy. I've got a few minutes to quickly check and reply to emails before I have a weekly supervision session with my trainee. I really like this time, as it feels like I'm contributing to the future of clinical psychology, but it also helps to consolidate my knowledge and challenges my practice. The day finishes with a therapy session using CBT and narrative therapy to help someone with anxiety. This makes all the meetings bearable, and shows what we are working for – to improve young people's quality of life and well-being. Back to the computer for the clinical notes and a few emails. I'll maybe do some journal reading at home, or maybe not. Sometimes there just isn't enough time!

Older adults: Many people aged over 65 will receive psychological interventions from the mainstream psychological therapy services provided for adults. People can continue to experience the whole range of psychological distress as they get older but there is a range of psychological issues that are particularly associated with ageing, e.g. dementia, and the impact of chronic physical health problems, and when individuals present with such difficulties, more specialist services are required, provided by clinicians with particular areas of expertise.

A clinical psychologist working with older people

I think that the word I use most frequently when asked to describe being a clinical psychologist working with older people is "variety". There are many occasions and situations when I ask myself "how have I ended up doing this?" but for me the variety and unexpected nature of the work is why I love it. Working with older people (generally considered as over 65, although this may vary from to service to service, and a number of people at 65 and over don't consider themselves older) you encounter many of the issues you would come across in a working age population, such as anxiety, low mood, unusual experiences and beliefs and difficulties associated with past traumas. In these situations I might work with people on an individual basis using a variety of psychological models based on the specific issues the person is facing. In addition I find that many of the older people I work with are facing transitions in their lives, such as retirement, living with a physical health condition or bereavement, which can add an extra dimension to the work. As such, you find yourself supporting people through some very difficult and emotional times in their lives.

The other side of my work is supporting people living with dementia. Until relatively recently it was believed that, apart from neuropsychological assessment, clinical psychology did not have a role to play in dementia services. Fortunately that view has changed and a large part of my role is working with people living with dementia and those who support them to live as well as possible with the condition. Whilst one aspect of this involves undertaking neuropsychological assessments to help with the process of diagnosing dementia and identifying cognitive strengths, much of my work in dementia services now focuses on working both with individuals and groups to facilitate adjustment to the diagnosis and the ongoing changes that take place whilst living with dementia. I recently undertook a piece of work with people living with dementia to find out what they wanted from psychology. What came across strongly was that they value being given the time and space to explore the changes that are happening to them and their families and ultimately this gave a sense of empowerment to continuing living their life in a successful way. For me that is what clinical psychology is all about!

People who have intellectual (learning) disabilities: People who have learning disabilities experience the same range of emotional and psychological difficulties as those who do not and, in fact, are more likely than other groups of people to experience psychological distress and mental health difficulties. This is probably due to a combination of factors, including an increased likelihood of sensory and neurological disability; a lack of close and meaningful relationships; increased vulnerability to experiences of loss and trauma and reduced access to sources of support and to things that build resilience. Clinical psychologists often have to adapt therapeutic approaches in order for these to be most useful for people with learning disabilities.

Day in the life of a clinical psychologist working in a community adult learning disability service

8.30 – checking emails, admin, reviewing a Positive Behaviour Support Plan for a client.

9.20 – care coordinator work for client – analysing incident forms to work out why she has begun to show high levels of self-injury – could be related to epilepsy, but she's also got some health problems that might be causing her pain so I have referred her for some health checks. Might also be links with environmental or social factors.

10.00 – discussion about a new referral for someone who has come to the UK as a refugee from the Democratic Republic of Congo but doesn't speak any English. We have to work out whether he is already known to our service or needs an assessment of whether he has a learning disability.

10.20 – meeting to plan a service specification for someone who has severe autism and highly complex needs that make it a challenge to support him well.

12.10 – lunch, discussion with social worker about a referral for someone who has become very distressed after a recent bereavement – staff need guidance about how to support him.

12.30 – preparing for home visit to someone who gets very angry and upset and shows this by hitting out at staff. We have been working to find out what causes him to feel angry and help him express it differently and also for staff to communicate better with him. I am worried that sometimes they are leaving him alone and he is becoming bored so I want to talk about why it is important that he has interesting enjoyable things to do.

12.55 – phone call from another psychologist to confer about a client who was being physically held by staff – we think that there might be less restrictive ways of ensuring his safety.

13.00 – 1:1 assessment session re: mental health. P has been hearing voices and seeing things that other people can't see and he has become very upset about this.

2.15 – update discussion with nurse re: a client with a forensic history – he has committed serious sexual assault against children in the past and spent some time in a special hospital. He has been resettled into the community and we are working on understanding the risks he now presents and ensuring there is a robust risk management plan in place.

2.30 – work on an intensive observation of a client by a colleague – we are trying to understand her self-injurious behaviour so have been observing her at different times and in different environments. Arrange an MDT [multidisciplinary team] meeting with colleagues. Quick look at some training I am running tomorrow about autism.

3.00 – scoring up measures and finishing clinical notes. One of them is a repeat assessment of cognitive skills for someone who has Downs

Syndrome. We screen everyone with Downs Syndrome regularly because they are more likely to develop dementia than other groups of people so we need to ensure it is spotted quickly so appropriate medication and support can be put in place.

4.30 – supervision session with a trainee on placement with me – she is coming towards the end of her placement so we talked about ensuring that all her clients understood she was leaving and the issues that this might raise for them. She showed me some of the letters she has written and adapted for clients with different levels of understanding – there was a great one with some pictures and an audio recording.

Neuropsychology: Clinical psychologists working in neuropsychology work with people whose lives are affected by changes in their brains, either due to sudden and acute causes, such as stroke, an accident or illness, or more gradually by, for example, dementia or lifelong conditions such as epilepsy. The role can be focused on complex neuropsychological assessment, or rehabilitation, or both (depending on the service).

A day in the life of a clinical neuropsychologist working across two very different services

In my role within adult mental health, I provide neuropsychological assessments for clients with severe mental illness who have cognitive changes and may have coexisting neurological conditions. This part of the job tends to be predictable and well planned, and affords me time to think, plan and prepare. I see clients at an outpatient clinic for interview and cognitive testing, with sessions lasting up to two hours. After this there's always the scoring and interpretation of the tests to do (i.e. number crunching), and the sometimes-lengthy report writing process. I might liaise with other mental health staff who are supporting the client and I will always arrange to feedback to the client. Sometimes I may be asked to see clients on inpatient mental health wards as well. I also get involved in service development projects and am always looking for opportunities to improve the visibility of neuropsychology within the Trust.

Conversely my two days on an acute stroke rehabilitation unit are unpredictable and fast paced, as I have to respond to the needs of patients who may only be on the ward for a few days. I am lucky enough to work with an assistant psychologist, so a typical day will start with supervision to catch up on existing and new referrals. Referrals usually relate to patients who are struggling to engage in rehabilitation, or who the other therapists are "stuck" with. I will see any patients as and when I can, trying to catch them between medical reviews, other therapy sessions and personal care. Mostly I see people at their bedside, which brings a whole host of challenges we don't experience in outpatient settings. I might assess cognitive functioning, or emotional well-being, or just have a conversation to see where the person is at. Sometimes I am asked to assess capacity to make a specific decision. Clear communication with the rest of the Multi-Disciplinary Team (MDT) is vital in this role, and this might be done through MDT meetings, written guidelines or just an informal conversation. There are also family meetings to attend when needed. In this role I get asked to do lots of staff training, which I really enjoy.

Physical health: There is a close and complex link between our psychological and physical health and there are many clinical psychologists who work with people who have physical health difficulties. You will often find clinical psychologists working with people with long-term conditions such as kidney disorder, diabetes and autoimmune disorders as well as more sudden onset conditions; burns; oncology (cancer); pain; stroke; bariatrics (obesity) assessment for surgery; and conditions associated with particular life events – pre-, peri- and post-natal maternity care and in palliative (end of life) care.

A day in the life of being a clinical psychologist working into an NHS cancer service

A typical day will include both direct and indirect work in ensuring the emotional and psychological well-being of people affected by cancer is prioritised. My own role requires me to work directly with people who are struggling emotionally either to deal with the impact of their cancer diagnosis, the impact of their cancer treatments (such as chemotherapy or surgery), and in some cases the impact of being told that their cancer is not curable. A typical day can involve seeing people at all the different stages of the cancer pathway – from early diagnosis to end-of-life issues.

I work within a multidisciplinary environment with colleagues from different professional backgrounds such as medicine and nursing. The skills I have developed as a clinical psychologist include being able to provide expert psychological consultation and formulation around cases that my colleagues ask for help with. For example, I may be consulted by a nursing colleague on how they should support a patient who they have to give bad news to because a recent scan has shown that their cancer has spread.

Clinical psychologists also provide training and supervision to other professional staff working in cancer around improving their skills in offering emotional and psychological support. Being able to provide psychological "first-aid" is expected from all staff who come in contact with patients and it is important that we ensure the staff feel confident in doing so.

My job is frequently demanding and requires me to practice good self-care because of how often I have to work with high levels of distress, particularly around dealing with death and dying. Sadly, many of the people I work with will eventually die as a result of their cancer. I make sure I always access regular support and supervision from fellow clinical psychologists.

Forensic: This refers to working with people who have committed crimes or are at risk of doing so. There are many psychologists who work with offenders out in the community but also in prisons. Some people who commit offences and who have mental health problems are treated in secure (high, medium or low) special hospitals rather than prison, and clinical psychologists are often among the staff who support and offer interventions to those people. Whereas clinical psychologists often are employed to work in forensic services, it is also possible to train as a forensic psychologist and we suggest you look at the book in this series for more detailed information about this.

There are also clinical psychologists employed in other statutory services, such as education or charities, who will provide care that is free to the recipient at the point of access. Clinical psychologists will also work in higher education in research and academic posts and you can see examples of such roles in Chapter 6.

Clinical psychologists working in private practice

Whilst the large majority of clinical psychologists are employed to work in the NHS, some also have a private practice in their own time, and a small number work entirely in private practice – though this number may be increasing. These clinical psychologists are self-employed and work alone or have joined together in small companies or social enterprises. Sometimes people choose to do this because they want to decide their own working hours and conditions and they can choose how much they charge the people they see. Some clinicians argue that they can earn a higher salary by working privately, that it is a more flexible and less constrained way of practising.

The disadvantages of working privately might include the potential lack of colleagues and the opportunities associated with working in a large organisation, as well as the work required to organise your own supervision, administration, continuing professional development, finances, tax and accounts and pressures relating to lack of sick pay and the potential need for a private pension. In order to work in private practice, a clinical psychologist must maintain their registration with the HCPC.

A day in the life of a clinical psychologist working in private practice

My clinic days usually start at 8 am and finish around 7.45 pm. Like most psychologists in private practice, I rent a consulting room by the day. I work in central London where room rates are very high so I need to make the most of my day. I have three clinic days each week and do my administration during one of the other days, unless I have a gap in the day and attend to my phone calls. I also do some follow-ups by phone, Facetime or Skype from home.

After qualifying as a clinical psychologist I worked in the NHS for several years mainly in primary care. I started working in private practice when I had young children as I needed to be able to be flexible with my hours of work. Much of my clinical work is similar to what I was doing in the NHS in primary care. In private practice we often don't know what kind of difficulties clients are having before they arrive, and we need to be able to work with a wide range of presentations. I work with adults, some as young as 18 either in their final year of school or starting university up to those in their 70s.

Almost every day, I will be speaking with a GP or a psychiatrist about clients I might be worried about. I would try and do this during a clinic day. I work independently but have a psychiatrist that I work very closely with. We share many clients and I will often have an opportunity to speak with him during the day, between patients. If people are being seen privately, they expect to be seen quickly and at a time that suits them. Many of my clients have very demanding jobs and therefore like to be seen either first thing in the morning or after work, so invariably the 8 am and 6 and 7 pm slots are in high demand.

Each session is 55 to 60 minutes long and as I take notes during the session, I will complete these and write back to the referrer on an admin day. Every day I check my resources such as forms and handouts. I get to work about 7.45 am, give my list to the receptionist and have a quick cup of tea before starting.

Yesterday, my first client was at 8 am and I finished at 7 pm. I saw a variety of clients, a young married man with two young children struggling with chronic depression and OCD and in recovery from alcohol dependence. This was followed by telephone consultations with two university students who I saw for intensive anxiety management work during the summer holidays. I met with a woman with a chronic history of substance abuse and sexually compulsive behaviour following a traumatic childhood. She was one year sober yesterday and I meet with her twice a week.

In summary I would say that there are many advantages to private practice, such as flexibility and pay. I can meet with clients for as many sessions as they need. However, it can be highly pressurising and lonely at times. The things I miss most about my work in the NHS are working in a team, peer support, training opportunities, variability and not worrying about work drying out. I feel privileged about my training as a clinical psychologist and remember my NHS days with joy, but would I change my decision to go into private work? not for one moment!

How much are clinical psychologists paid?

Clinical psychologists who work within the NHS are usually paid on the standard NHS pay scales that were agreed under the Agenda for Change framework that unified the terms and conditions for many of the staff working in the NHS. You can find out up to date salaries associated with the different grades on the NHS Employers website* (www.nhsemployers.org).

Assistant Psychologist – Band 4 (£20,150 to £23,363) or Band 5 (£23,032 to £29,608)
Trainee Clinical Psychologist – Band 6 (£28,050 to £36,644)
Newly qualified Clinical Psychologist – Band 7 (£33,222 to £43,041)
Senior and Consultant Clinical Psychologists – Bands 8a–d (£42,414 to £85,333)

Clinical psychologists working in academic posts are usually paid on university clinical/academic pay scales. Clinical psychologists who work privately can decide how much to charge. Clinical psychologists working in other services, such as education or for charities, will be paid dependent on that organisation's pay scales, but their salary is likely to be similar to the NHS salaries.

How much does it cost to train to be a clinical psychologist?

Most UK trainee clinical psychologists are salaried employees of the NHS on Band 6 (Agenda for Change – starting salary in 2018 was £28,050). The NHS also pays the university tuition fees. A minority of UK programmes offer self-funded places, and details of these can be found on the Clearing House for Postgraduate Courses in Clinical Psychology website (https://chpccp.leeds.ac.uk/) and on the university websites of the individual programmes. The Clearing House for Postgraduate Courses in Clinical Psychology manages the applications to clinical psychology training programmes at 30 UK universities. It is a registered non-profit educational charity working with clinical psychology courses to provide information and an easy to use application system.

There has been uncertainty about the future funding of clinical psychology training in England since the government's Comprehensive Spending Review announcement in November 2015. This led to a decision by the UK government to end NHS funding in England of a number of health care programmes, including nursing, midwifery and the allied health professions – with funding shifting from Health Education England to the Student Loans system. At the time of this book going to print, clinical psychology training in England continues to be funded through the NHS (Health Education England) but this may be subject to change.

We would strongly recommend that when you are considering studying at university you find out about the many different awards and bursaries that are available. Most universities will have "widening participation" awards that aim to encourage a diverse range of students to attend – especially those who come from families that have not previously attended university and students who have disabilities or students experiencing financial hardship. These awards and bursaries are usually additional to the student loans that cover tuition fees and maintenance and do not have to be paid back. Check with each individual university whether you might be entitled to any such awards, as it can make a huge difference to the financial decision about undergraduate studies.

Why do you want to be a clinical psychologist?

We have found it to be useful and interesting for people considering clinical psychology to hear from other people who have also considered it and decided to proceed or not. We asked a range of people some questions about what they liked and disliked about their jobs as clinical psychologists. One qualified clinical psychologist colleague shares advice about being sure that this is the career for you: "*Think about why you would want to do this job – what is pulling you to such a niche career when you could make more money doing something easier?*" The following may help to guide you.

What are the best things about being a clinical psychologist?

It's always interesting – I've never had two days the same and I like that. I would hate to be in a job that I did the same things over and over again. Even if two referrals look almost the same on paper, the two people who show up will be completely different.

(Qualified clinical psychologist)

It's a privilege to be with people when they are at their most distressed and vulnerable and you have to take that responsibility very seriously. You are sometimes the first or only person who someone has ever been able to talk to about something important that has happened to them and that is a real privilege.

(Qualified clinical psychologist)

The best aspects are when you think you've helped someone in some way. Just being warm, listening, and showing empathy can be life changing for someone who has never experienced this. It's a privilege to hear people's stories.

(Year 3 trainee)

I have heard people tell me their stories that include the worst things I could have imagined but I have also seen how people survive and are resilient and that has taught me so much about people and what they are capable of and about myself.

(Year 2 trainee clinical psychologist)

I work with adults with autism and I have met some of the most interesting, talented, funny and wonderful people that you can imagine.

(Qualified clinical psychologist)

It is a job that requires you to be a thoughtful scientist and to use evidence and best practice to help people – it's so much more rigorous than some other "helping" jobs and I like that.

(Trainee clinical psychologist)

It is quite a well-paid job compared to lots of others in the NHS and although it took a long time to train and I have lots of responsibilities I don't ever feel like I am on my own.

(Newly qualified clinical psychologist)

I have great colleagues – it is really important to me to work in the NHS.

(Qualified clinical psychologist)

I work in a university as an academic and also in the NHS and I am excited that I can combine both. The things that my research is finding out will have real-life implications and applications in the future.

(Qualified clinical psychologist and lecturer)

You have to be creative – I like thinking about how I am going to help children understand complicated ideas in a way that will make sense to them.

(Year 3 trainee)

We also asked about the worst and most challenging things about the job:

It can be exhausting – sometimes I am completely drained and haven't got any energy left for my family. I try really hard to balance work and home, but it's a real challenge.

(Qualified clinical psychologist)

The politics of the NHS or the university can make it hard to get things done and I can see the impact of the cuts in services on my patients and colleagues and don't know what to do about it.

(Qualified clinical psychologist and clinical tutor)

Although I like working privately because I can fit it round my other commitments, I do get lonely and miss having colleagues and worry about my financial future.

(Qualified clinical psychologist)

Transferring from another career

We come across a lot of people who have changed from one career to become clinical psychologists; sometimes they have come from a related field, such as educational psychology, medicine, nursing, counselling or social work, and on other occasions from entirely different careers, including accountancy, catering, musician, police work and banking. There are advantages and disadvantages of changing career to become a clinical psychologist:

Would you recommend transferring from another profession?

> *Yes, definitely – clinical psychology is a profession where you can make a real difference in people's lives and it is always interesting.*
>
> (Year 2 trainee)

> *People who have previous professions often bring really helpful new perspectives and experiences to their training. The profession always benefits from having a wide range of people in it.*
>
> (Clinical tutor)

> *The training is tough and can be hard to balance with family life but often the people who have had other professions manage this really well.*
>
> (Clinical tutor)

> *It's really hard to begin again and feel like you are just starting out at the bottom of a career structure all over again.*
>
> (Year 2 trainee)

> *Yes, I had always been frustrated that I couldn't use my psychology background and it is the most interesting job I could imagine so I'm glad I took a risk and made the change.*
>
> (Newly qualified clinical psychologist)

What comes next

Having described what clinical psychology is and is not, how it differs from related fields of work and what it involves, the rest of this book describes the educational requirements needed to apply for clinical psychology training, the types of work experience available, how to apply for a training programme and information about the selection process, a description of what is involved in clinical psychology training, what it is like to work when newly qualified and some of the career routes available once qualified.

Endnotes

* All salary figures are taken from the Agenda for Change salary scales for England from 1st April 2018.

3

The psychology graduate

Chapter 1 of this book addressed some of the questions that you may have if you are at the early stages of considering a career in a field of psychology:

- Which A-levels should I take if I want to study psychology at university?
- How many universities offer psychology undergraduate courses?
- Are some university psychology degrees better than others? How do I choose?
- What if I have a psychology degree from a university outside of the UK and Ireland?
- Do you need to go to a particular university to do a psychology degree?

In this chapter we focus on what you need to consider specifically in relation to clinical psychology as a career option. We describe the educational and relevant work experience requirements for applying for clinical psychology training and provide hints and tips on how to navigate the process of applying for training. We also pass on some advice about work experience from people who have succeeded in getting places on training programmes.

Which qualifications do you need to apply for clinical psychology training?

Clinical psychology training in the UK is at doctoral level and requires a high level of educational attainment over a number of years. In order to apply, you will usually need an undergraduate degree in psychology. Other degrees may also be acceptable; such as joint honours degrees (where you study psychology and another subject), or a different degree with a conversion course. It is essential that the undergraduate degree confers Graduate Basis for Chartered Membership (GBC) with the British Psychological Society (BPS) (see Chapter 1 for details). Applicants for clinical training often have a Master's or PhD degree too, but these are not essential requirements (see later section on Master's and PhD degrees). People applying to clinical psychology training programmes in the UK also need to have acquired some relevant work experience.

Is it worth taking a psychology degree that has a focus on clinical psychology?

People who are considering pursuing clinical training frequently ask whether it is important to do a psychology degree that has an emphasis on clinical psychology. There is a very high demand for clinical psychology training places in the UK (in 2018 there were 3866 applications to the UK Clearing House for Postgraduate Courses in Clinical Psychology and a total of 593 places offered – 15% success rate). So if you are seriously thinking that this may be the career for you, you might be considering opting for an undergraduate course that has more clinical content and/or to pick one that offers work placements. Our advice is that whilst this might be helpful, it is certainly not essential. In order to be a clinical psychologist it is necessary to have a good grounding in psychology in general, hence the need to have a degree that confers GBC with the BPS. If you apply for a course that offers clinical psychology options this may help you to gain an idea of what clinical psychology is about and how you can apply your psychological knowledge to clinical populations. Doing a course that has clinical content, with taught input from clinical psychologists, may help you to gain an idea of clinical psychology as a profession and of the type of work undertaken by clinical psychologists. Likewise, opting for a degree that offers clinical work placements may help you to decide whether this is the career for you. However, whilst it is important to demonstrate that you have a keen interest in clinical psychology throughout your studies and work (voluntary or paid) experience, this is not essential at this early stage. Choice of degree course with clinical psychology content is not generally a factor that the programmes give weight to when considering applications from candidates applying for clinical psychology training.

Is it worth looking at courses that offer a work placement? Are the placements worthwhile?

As discussed in Chapter 1, whilst looking for possible degree courses, it might be worth checking out those that offer work placements, though this is not essential. A number of UK universities offer the opportunity to do a year-long work placement, including clinical placements. These universities offer four-year psychology degrees which include a placement year that has an emphasis on real-world applications of psychology. Students still pay fees to the university (albeit reduced) during the placement year.

In many ways, the experience gained during an undergraduate degree placement year is similar to that gained as a voluntary assistant psychologist, which we will discuss later in this chapter. However, placements do not suit everyone, as they require students to be able to afford to spend a year without receiving any salary whilst still paying reduced university fees. We have spoken with people who have found their placements very valuable and others who did not feel they gained anything from them at all.

Here are some accounts and opinions from people who had placement experience:

An undergraduate psychology student reflected on her experience of a work placement: "*My placement in SW London has been a real eye-opener to the reality of clinical psychology as well as the ways the NHS works and also very enjoyable and rewarding experience, which I'm very grateful for*".

A Year 1 trainee clinical psychologist, interviewed for this book, reflected on her experience of doing a placement which started at the end of her second year of her undergraduate psychology degree. She did a full-time nine-month placement, on an honorary (unpaid) contract, in an NHS Child and Adolescent Mental Health Service

(CAMHS). She recalls that the university gave her a total of approximately £1000 but that she had to pay her own expenses for the duration of the placement. The breadth of her work was relatively limited due to this having been an honorary position. She recalls doing lots of administrative work, such as printing and producing materials and resources for clinicians to use. She was, however, given many opportunities to shadow a range of different CAMHS professionals as well as a number of clinical psychologists working in different roles. She feels that the most useful aspect of this placement experience was gaining a sense of inter-professional working, getting a good idea of what a clinical psychologist does and developing networks. Looking back, she feels that undergraduate degree placements can be a good stepping stone to other sorts of relevant work for a career in clinical psychology. She subsequently secured a university research assistant post and was told that having done the undergraduate placement had helped her to stand out during the recruitment process as it was viewed as being good relevant work experience.

A current undergraduate psychology student did a placement as part of her course in an NHS mental health trust in London that was helpful in her decision not to pursue clinical psychology. She describes the placement as having been "*a real eye-opener to the reality of clinical psychology as well as the ways in which the NHS works and also a very enjoyable and rewarding experience*". She facilitated three psychoeducational groups for patients, took part in a reflecting team in a family therapy clinic and organised and ran a relaxation group for the patients on an acute mental health ward. This was a placement that offered a wide variety of experiences that were all highly relevant to gaining a place on a clinical psychology training programme. The student recalls enjoying the placement and recommends students doing similar placements if considering a career in clinical psychology. For this student, however, working alongside trainee clinical psychologists whilst doing her placement made her aware of the challenges, particularly personal and financial, of training:

> *Hearing about how long and hard the journey is to becoming a clinical psychologist put me off slightly, but the cost of it all was what made me really reconsider going down that route. . . . Nevertheless, I have not completely dismissed the idea of becoming a clinical psychologist,*

> *as it is such a wonderful career. I will just have to explore more options and possibly find other ways of going about it.*

The advice that this student gives, based on her experience, is that if you are interested in clinical psychology as a career, you should "*network as much as possible and contact as many people as you can. I got my placement by finding a list of psychologists on the BPS website and emailing them – many didn't reply, a few were extremely helpful and gave me tonnes of information (which makes them very useful contacts to have) and one of them offered me a placement*". She concludes by saying "*definitely do a placement year if you have the chance. No matter what, it will benefit you in one way or another. If I hadn't done mine, I would be going on a long and very hard journey to becoming something, which I now know I'm not too sure about*".

Another Year 2 trainee clinical psychologist recalls how helpful it was to do a placement during their undergraduate degree:

> *I would encourage students to pursue a placement year during their degree if this is offered. Having completed one myself, it gave me the motivation to study harder in final year and also confirmed that clinical psychology is a career I'd like to pursue rather than a fantasy of what a clinical psychologist's role is and disliking this upon training/qualification.*

As you can see from these stories and advice, placements can be valuable experience but if you do choose to take on a work placement it is useful to consider what experience it will actually offer and whether it will be helpful to you.

Questions you may consider when applying for a degree that offers work placements:

- Will you have to find the placement yourself or will it be organised for you?
- Does the course guarantee that you will get a clinically related placement or will there be lots of students competing for those placements?
- What will the placement activity actually involve and have previous students found it to be worthwhile?

To reiterate, most clinical psychologists do not have undergraduate degrees that included work placements and you should not be put off if the psychology degree that most appeals to you does not include a placement opportunity. If you do decide to undertake a placement, try to ensure it will actually be valuable experience for you.

What undergraduate degree classification do I need to get if I want to become a clinical psychologist?

Given the competition for places and the academic demand of clinical psychology training, the main priority is getting a high 2:1 or 1st class honours degree.

A Year 2 trainee clinical psychologist recalls advice he wishes that he had been given early on: "*I would have benefitted from knowing that a high 2:1 is essential, with many course centres not accepting applicants if they have not achieved an average of 65%. Had I known this during my undergraduate degree I would have made more effort with my academic demands. I would also encourage A-level/undergraduate students to make the most of their limited responsibilities, increased time and more favourable finances to seek voluntary opportunities for experience. This is increasingly difficult to pursue and juggle following graduation and when you may need to work a full-time job*".

A Year 2 trainee clinical psychologist recalls doing her undergraduate degree and on what would have helped: "*I wish I had known how academically the chances of getting on are now much more pressured. I would have probably tried to get a higher degree and put more focus on gaining some clinical experience while studying*".

What if I don't get a 2:1 or 1st?

Although a 2:1 or 1st is a usually a requirement for acceptance onto clinical psychology training, there are people who have successfully been accepted with a 2:2 when they have gained a further postgraduate degree after their undergraduate studies – see the section on Master's and PhDs that follows.

After my psychology degree – what then? Do I need to do a Master's or PhD as well?

If you have now completed your psychology undergraduate degree, have secured a high 2:1 or 1st and are interested in pursuing a career as a clinical psychologist – what is next for you educationally? Under those circumstances, you do not need to gain further educational qualifications, although some people do choose to do so. If you have gained a 2:2 then you probably will need to gain a further academic degree. Some clinical psychology training programmes stipulate that applicants with a 2:2 for their undergraduate degree must have done a relevant Master's degree and achieved a merit or distinction in order to be considered for training. So, if you have completed your undergraduate psychology degree and have a 2:2, do consider doing a Master's if you can afford to do so. This is particularly helpful if you have a good reason for thinking that you would be able to attain a substantially higher grade in your Master's degree than you did for your undergraduate degree.

Successful candidates for training in clinical psychology are those that are able to understand and apply psychological theories and principles. Applicants need to be able to demonstrate that they have the ability to critically evaluate psychological literature and to conduct research independently to doctoral standard. To this end, many applicants for clinical psychology training in the UK have a higher academic qualification beyond their undergraduate degree which helps to give them the additional academic and research experience. In the majority of cases, this is a Master's degree.

Examples of the types of Master's degrees undertaken by applicants for UK clinical psychology training include:

- MRes Psychology
- MSc Clinical and Health Psychology
- MSc Forensic Psychology
- MSc Applied Psychology (Psychological Therapies)
- MSc Research Methods and Statistics
- MSc Psychological Therapies in Primary Care
- MSc Cognitive and Behavioural Therapies
- MSc Developmental Psychopathology

A number of applicants for clinical psychology training have completed a PhD and others may have additional qualifications in psychological therapy training such as a cognitive behaviour therapy (CBT) postgraduate certificate or diploma. There are pros and cons of undertaking further study before applying for clinical training and for those who already have been awarded a 2:1 for their undergraduate studies reasons for doing a Master's or PhD vary. Those employed as research assistants will often register for higher degrees as part of their paid work. For many, doing a Master's degree is part of strengthening their application for training. Bear in mind, however, that doing a further degree may be costly and that many applicants successfully gain places on clinical psychology training programmes with an undergraduate degree only, so the picture is somewhat mixed. The BPS's *Alternative Handbook for Postgraduate Training Course in Clinical Psychology* provides detailed information from current trainees on each programme, including how many hold postgraduate qualifications; see https://shop.bps.org.uk/.

Why is clinical psychology training different to other academic study?

The progression from GCSEs to A levels (or equivalents) is often quite a straightforward one. You already know whether you like being in the classroom and whether you enjoy learning in that way. You might have chosen to study A-level psychology or equivalent because you looked at the curriculum or attended a taster session, heard other people talk about it or just thought it sounded more interesting than the other subjects on offer. During A-level psychology, if the topics you have been studying have made you sufficiently interested to think about going on to study psychology at university, you will find that there are some aspects of undergraduate study that continue to feel familiar at university, such as attending lectures and reading, writing essays and taking exams. It is likely that you will already know where your academic strengths lie and what you find more difficult.

It is important to realise that there is a very large jump from completing an undergraduate degree to becoming a trainee clinical psychologist.

Even though some of the academic aspects are the same (lectures, essays and, sometimes, written exams), there is huge shift because, as a trainee, you will not only be completing academic study to a much higher level but also will be employed by the NHS, providing real clinical services to real people in the real world of work, with all of the challenges that this brings.

One of the ways that you can be best prepared for this transition is by gaining some work experience. This is an essential part of the process of becoming a clinical psychologist.

Why is getting work experience a good idea?

Gaining some relevant work experience is a good idea for a number of reasons:

- It helps you work out whether you suit this kind of job. For example, are you someone who can thrive and work effectively with people who at times are very distressed and may behave in ways that cause distress to others? Will you actually cope with working with people who are in psychological distress – something that is very different in reality than theory? Are you comfortable with adapting the ways you communicate to work effectively with people whose communication abilities are very different? Are you someone who is able to interact confidently with other adults in a workplace? Are you able to manage multiple demands and pressures of work in a competent and professional manner? The training programmes always want people who have had experience and are able to reflect and learn from it.
- It helps you become clearer about your strengths and the areas where you may need further skills development. Feedback from employers and colleagues can be valuable in this process. Work experience also helps you build up a sense of what you might want to do if you change your mind or decide that clinical psychology is not for you.
- Work experience will mean that you have good referees available when you apply for training. Applications have to include evidence from referees who have relevant knowledge about you and having work experience means that you can provide references that help

the clinical psychology programmes decide whether to shortlist you and invite you for an interview.

Should I look for relevant work experience before, during or after university?

We would recommend that, whatever your stage of education, once you are considering pursuing clinical psychology as a career, you start trying to get some relevant work experience. Even short periods of work experience such as a couple of weeks out of term time or a regular evening commitment can be interesting and useful and demonstrate your commitment to this choice of career.

A newly qualified clinical psychologist advises that, if you are considering a career as a clinical psychologist, then "*Whilst at university perhaps see if you can become involved with research that the department is doing or volunteer jobs with help lines or work as a health care assistant*". A qualified clinical psychologist recalls: "*At the same time as I was doing my A-levels and degree, I did a mixture of paid work (retail) and unpaid work. It was the unpaid work that proved beneficial – I worked with Occupational Therapists helping people to rehabilitate back to the community after their stay in hospital*".

Finding relevant work experience

A great place to start to find relevant work experience is at your school, college or university; most will have a careers service that will be able to advise you and link you with work agencies and volunteering schemes. There are many types of work experience, but one of the important distinctions is whether it is voluntary or paid.

Voluntary work experience

Voluntary experience is work in an unpaid capacity – simply volunteering your time. There is a difference between being a voluntary worker (which has all the qualities and responsibilities of a paid job but without the wage) and a volunteer (when you give up your time to work without pay and without some of the other responsibilities that a worker would have). Lots of the people we talked to when writing this book had done some volunteering and described the advantages and disadvantages it offers.

The advantages include:

- It demonstrates that you are interested in and dedicated to your choice of future career.
- You can get a wide variety of work that you might not be able to get in paid positions.
- It will enable you to make links and connections in health and social care services, and sometimes volunteering leads to paid work in the same service.
- It will help you to understand how a range of different services work and sometimes you get to see how psychology fits in.
- You can fit voluntary work around other studies or paid work.
- You can easily leave if you do not like the work you are doing.

The main disadvantages of doing voluntary work experience:

- Not getting paid! That means that not everyone can afford to do it.
- There are not always the same protections as if it were a paid job so you have to be careful that your goodwill is not taken advantage of and that you are not asked to do things that you are not qualified or competent to do.
- When it comes to shortlisting for an interview on a clinical psychology programme, voluntary work is useful but not sufficient – it does not replace the requirement for paid work experience.

The BPS has published a position statement and good practice guidelines on Applied practitioner psychologist internship programmes and unpaid voluntary assistant psychologist posts (BPS, 2018).

Many of the trainees and clinical psychologists who have contributed their experiences to this book undertook voluntary work or volunteering along the way to securing a place on clinical psychology training. For example, a Year 2 trainee sums this up by saying: "*I don't believe you should have to volunteer full-time, but showing an awareness of the different areas that clinical psychologists work in (by experiencing them) did me so much good. I volunteered in a clinical psychology research department, while working as a carer with the elderly and at Rape Crisis on an evening".*

What's the best sort of voluntary work experience?

The best sorts of work experience are those that give you a chance to work with different kinds of people. Lots of people who apply for training have worked as care assistants/health care assistants/support workers, as assistants in schools or care homes, or in charities for people with mental health or physical disabilities. Many UK schools and colleges run Duke of Edinburgh schemes (www.dofe.org/) that include an aspect of community work. Other organisations that you might consider when looking for voluntary work experience include the National Citizen Service (www.ncsyes.co.uk/) and the National Council for Voluntary Organisations (NCVO) (www.ncvo.org.uk/).

It is important to remember that any kind of work experience, voluntary or paid, will require some skills that are relevant for clinical psychology training even though they may not be immediately apparent. Working in a shop or café, a warehouse, a supermarket or a call centre may feel a long way from clinical psychology-related work but you may be getting good experience of being in a professional workplace, taking instruction, interacting in an adult role, dealing with the public (who at times can be upset, angry, demanding and challenging) demonstrating timekeeping and other work-related skills. Do not underestimate the value of such work experience. Once you are at university you will find that many universities have extremely good opportunities and schemes for getting voluntary (and paid) work experience as they recognise the value this can add to the employability of their students.

> *It's great if someone has experience of a range of voluntary work – probably better than just working in psychology because they have demonstrated enthusiasm and commitment and have probably had a really wide range of different experiences that they will be bringing.*
>
> (Clinical psychology training programme director)

Don't stick with just one thing – if possible get as wide a range of experience as possible. Some jobs offer this – with others you simply have to move on.

(Trainee clinical psychologist)

It's fine to be cheeky and approach places where you think you might get good experience. You have nothing to lose if they say "No" and it is good practise at being confident, and they might say "Yes"!

(Qualified clinical psychologist)

Paid work experience

Many people gain their most useful work experience after their undergraduate degree and, of course, most people will need to seek paid employment at that stage.

Assistant psychologist jobs

Perhaps the type of paid employment most obviously relevant to clinical psychology is an assistant psychologist post; these posts can provide excellent ways of developing clinical skills in real NHS (or NHS-commissioned) psychology services. Assistant posts that are based with qualified clinical psychologists can be particularly useful in allowing you to get to know more about the profession and make good links.

They are usually paid at Band 4 or 5 on the NHS's Agenda for Change pay scales (www.nhsemployers.org/your-workforce/pay-and-reward/agenda-for-change/pay-scales/annual). However, applications for these posts are extremely competitive and often some relevant experience is required before you are considered. Due to this, applications for these posts may close well before their publicised closing date, as employers will stop taking applications once a certain number has been reached.

The BPS's *Guidelines for Clinical Psychology Services* (BPS, 2011) includes guidance about the recruitment, responsibilities and roles of assistant psychologists and the support and supervision required by those roles.

What do assistant psychologists actually do?

The sorts of jobs that assistant psychologists do are almost as varied as those done by qualified clinical psychologists and you will find assistant posts in many psychology services. Ideally assistant psychology posts will be supervised by a clinical psychologist, but this is not always the case. Assistants are sometimes employed to work on designated projects, such as running particular therapy groups or carrying out specific assessments, whereas other assistant psychologists have wide-ranging and varied roles and will be involved in many aspects of assessment formulation and intervention under the supervision of a qualified staff member.

My job is to undertake interviews and neuropsychological assessments with people who have learning disabilities and their families and carers. We do these assessments because we know that people with learning disabilities are more likely to develop dementia than other people so we make sure everyone has a baseline assessment of their cognitive abilities so if there is any change we can spot it early enough to give medication and other support.

(Assistant psychologist)

I did an assistant psychology post that mainly seemed to involve spending time inputting clinical data onto a computer system, which was truly boring. The advantage was that I did eventually get to be involved in other work that the clinical psychologists were doing but it took a while.

(Qualified clinical psychologist)

How do you get an assistant psychologist post?

Many assistant psychologist posts will be advertised via NHS jobs (www.jobs.nhs.uk/) or via the BPS (www.jobsinpsychology.co.uk/). As assistant psychologist posts are easy to fill, many services will recruit locally and, as noted earlier, only advertise for a very short time. To find out about posts, it can be worth knowing where your local clinical psychology services are based. There is likely to be a local mental health trust where there may be a clinical psychology department, but other clinical psychologists will be based in hospitals, universities or community settings. An internet search of psychology services in your local area is a good way of starting to locate local clinical psychology services and it can be a worthwhile strategy to send a letter/email with your CV expressing interest in any posts that might be coming up. Some services recruit volunteer assistant psychologists so it is worth checking this out too.

Many areas of the country have assistant psychologists' networks that can be valuable sources of information about where and when posts might become available. More broadly, the BPS's DCP's Pre-Qualification Group is a valuable resource too (www1.bps.org.uk/networks-and-communities/member-microsite/division-clinical-psychology/prequalification-group).

> *Even though the jobs are competitive, don't behave like it's a competition. Treat other assistants as colleagues – there can be a friendly network that is supportive and helpful to you all.*
>
> (Trainee clinical psychologist)

It is useful to know that July to September is often a good time of year to be looking for assistant psychology posts, because those assistant psychologists who have been successful at getting places on the training courses leave their jobs to begin training.

Some of the people we talked to for this book gave the following advice about assistant psychologist jobs:

> *Try and make sure that you get as much experience as you can. Even if the job description is fairly limited you can often show willing and get involved in all kinds of things.*
>
> (Qualified clinical psychologist)

> *Don't be afraid to ask clinical psychologists for their help and advice about getting onto the course – they are often very happy to help.*
>
> (Clinical tutor)

> *If you want to get onto a training programme, don't stay in one assistant job for too long; the broader your experience the more likely*

you are to get offered an interview. Also try to get both clinical and research experience. Sometimes you can get involved in service research and get your name on a published article which is great for your CV.
(Clinical tutor)

There is great value in what you do before training – and it should not feel like a race to get on. Enjoy being an assistant, try as much as you can and don't make life all about getting onto the course because it is just one part of a wider journey.
(Year 2 trainee clinical psychologist)

The number of assistant psychology posts has been somewhat in decline in recent years and these jobs are tough to get, but there are many other relevant sources of work experience, so do not despair if you are not able to get work as an assistant psychologist – most people don't!

Research assistant posts

As with assistant psychologist jobs, research assistant posts can be highly sought after. Research assistants are usually employed by university departments for a fixed period of time to work as part of a team on a particular piece of research. They can be particularly valuable if there is an opportunity to be involved in the design of the research project and if there is the opportunity to be part of writing up and publication afterwards.

Research assistant posts are often related to particular funded research programmes being undertaken in clinical or health psychology departments in universities, so it is worth making contact with your local universities to find out about those posts and where they are advertised (www.jobs.ac.uk/).

PhD

A PhD (Doctor of Philosophy) is a postgraduate degree awarded to an individual following the submission of an extensive piece of original research. It usually takes three to four years of full-time study and often follows an undergraduate and master's degree. A minority of people gain a PhD before starting their clinical psychology training. This is not common, however, and we would not especially recommend it for most people as it is a lengthy process and very often does not involve a significant amount of clinical experience. Some clinical psychologists who go on to work in academic fields after qualifying will undertake a PhD post-qualification.

A recently qualified clinical psychologist shares her experience that includes both research assistant and PhD experience:

> *When I finished my undergraduate degree, I didn't really know what I wanted to do. . . . I knew that I was really interested in the clinical side of psychology, and so I wanted to get some experience of working clinically with people with mental health difficulties to see whether it felt like the right career path for me. I worked as a health care assistant in a secure forensic hospital for a couple of years, and, whilst working there, I was asked if I'd like to contribute to some research that was being done in the hospital. I said yes and quickly realised that I really enjoyed the challenge and excitement that clinical research brought, from recruiting participants down to analysing data and comparing the results with the findings of previous research studies. I felt like I had found my niche – something that I enjoyed, that had clear clinical applications and that I was (dare I say it!) good at.*
>
> *After much deliberation, I applied for a full-time research post at a university near to me. It was fixed-term for a year – which was a bit nerve wracking – and I felt like I was turning my back on clinical work, but I felt as though the benefits outweighed the uncertainty, and so when I was offered the post I immediately accepted it. After that post ended I quickly found another at a different university, which was also fixed-term. By then I had decided that I wanted a career in research, at least in some capacity, so I applied for a part-time, clinically focused PhD, which I completed alongside my day job.*
>
> *I thoroughly enjoyed the challenge of a PhD – and it was very challenging at times! – and especially enjoyed critically engaging with research findings and recruiting patients to my research. But the little voice in the back of my head was still there, reminding me that I really enjoyed working clinically with people too. At the end of my four-year*

PhD journey, my mind was made up. I didn't want to solely be a researcher. . . . I wanted to be an academic clinical psychologist. I completed one final fixed-term research contract, and then was accepted onto the Doctorate in Clinical Psychology programme.

My background helped me enormously on the programme. . . . I felt prepared for the academic components of the course, in part because I knew that I had previously managed to successfully complete a thesis, and therefore could (hopefully!) manage it a second time.

Because of my research background, I found some aspects of the course more challenging than others in my year. I was used to dedicating all of my time to one research project, so I initially found it difficult to balance all of the competing demands of the programme. My previous research roles were very relaxed, and I found it challenging to adjust to a more scheduled timetable, and to effectively organise clinic slots, meetings, lectures and research time each week. I also doubted myself a lot – I felt that my clinical knowledge was perhaps less than others in my year, and I found myself wondering whether they had made a mistake in letting me onto the course! I had to do a lot of reading, particularly when starting new placements, and it took a while for me to feel confident working clinically with people. However, I quickly adjusted to the new role.

What if I can't get an assistant or research psychologist post?

There are lots of other paid jobs that will give you experience that is directly relevant to applying for clinical psychology training and will stand you in good stead for making applications. We are aware of people who have successfully gained places on training courses having only worked in fields that have apparently little to do with clinical psychology but have acquired relevant qualities and skills.

After my degree, I had jobs working in a residential school for children with complex needs and challenging behaviours, working for a disability organisation as an information worker (which was extremely useful as it enabled me to learn how to work with people using plain language, translating information to meet the needs of people, especially those with learning disability) and finally working in a forensic hospital

(Qualified clinical psychologist)

If possible, try to find a job where there are clinical psychologists working there. Even if you aren't supervised by one, you can still learn a lot about how they work from being around them

(Year 1 trainee clinical psychologist)

See if you can shadow a clinical psychologist at some point, even for a day. Find out about what clinical psychologists do. . . . Is there an assistant psychologist /psychology interest group in your area? I joined one when I was an undergraduate, and eventually started running it. If there isn't one, could you start one? This can be a great way of networking, and finding out more about different roles in clinical psychology.

(Year 3 trainee clinical psychologist)

Working in Improving Access to Psychological Therapies (IAPT) services

Many of the people who have been successful at getting places on clinical psychology training courses in recent years have worked in IAPT services which are often provided by NHS mental health services. IAPT is a national programme operating in England aimed at providing quick and easy access to a range of psychological therapies. This started as a way of trying to help people who were unable to work due to feeling particularly anxious or low in mood to receive treatment quickly to allow them to return to the workplace. Now IAPT services offer a range of psychological interventions, often based on cognitive behaviour therapy (CBT), and over the years the range of treatments offered and the issues covered have increased. There are two main types of job in IAPT services: Psychological Wellbeing Practitioners (PWPs) are trained to offer the first line of treatments and High Intensity Therapists (HITs), who are more experienced practitioners who receive further training to work with people presenting with more complex difficulties. Often people who wish to become clinical psychologists seek those posts, as they involve a good basic training in CBT approaches and give broad experience of working with a range of people presenting with a variety of psychological difficulties.

You can find out more about your local IAPT service, training and PWP jobs online and through NHS Jobs.

> *I thought that my work within IAPT would give me a head start on the training programme. It was useful to have had experience using CBT because I wasn't so anxious about that at the start of training, but I soon realised that the work I was doing as a trainee was quite different and more complex. I do think it is useful experience though.*
> (Year 3 trainee)

Advice about work experience

Whatever your stage and whatever work experience you are considering, it is worth bearing in mind the qualities and competencies needed to become a clinical psychologist and thinking about whether you will have the chance to demonstrate or learn them. Our advice would be not to worry if you are unable to obtain direct experience of working with a clinical psychologist or in a psychological service immediately; any jobs where you are working with people and have the opportunity to get good references are valuable. Try to avoid thinking about work experience as simply being a step on the route to getting a place on a training course. Rather, treat work experience as a valuable learning experience in itself; everything goes to helping you become a person with more skills to offer, and you simply never know what experiences and opportunities any sort of work experience will present.

Make it as easy as possible to respond quickly to any work experience opportunities that arise by keeping your CV updated. It is also a good idea to get a driving licence if you can: it opens up wider opportunities and you are likely to need to be able to drive if you get on a training programme – some programmes require you to have a valid UK driving licence at interview. Training programmes do make reasonable adjustments for trainees who are not able to drive as a result of disability but, if you can drive, it is likely to provide you with much more flexibility.

Tips for applying for work experience posts – applications and interviews

Whatever sort of job you are looking at, you should always read the job description and person specification carefully and check that you meet the essential criteria; do not waste time applying for things for which you do not have the essential skills.

When you fill in an application form make it easy for the reader to look at and read; you would be amazed how many applications are poorly laid out and unclearly written with lots of spelling and grammatical errors, which give a poor impression of the applicant's capabilities. Clearly demonstrate that you have the required experience and the essential qualifications and show that you have reflected on the value of this experience if there is the opportunity to do so. Also, if the job advert offers a visit or personal conversation with someone in the service, take up the opportunity. When you do speak to them show interest and enthusiasm and have some sensible questions to ask that demonstrate that you know what the job is and are genuinely interested in applying.

If you decide to apply for a job, or are invited for interview, make sure you have found out everything you can about the job and prepare your application and interview with the specific job in mind; do not just submit a generic application or turn up unsure about what the job actually entails. Find out what the interview will involve beforehand. If you are required to give a brief presentation it should tell you in the letter what the topic is, but make sure you know whether there will be audio-visual equipment and for how long you should present. Make sure you stay within the allocated amount of time for the presentation and, if in doubt, keep it simple to avoid having to fumble with technology when you are feeling nervous.

Interviews can range from those that feel very informal and chatty to those that are much more formal. Bear in mind that, however friendly the interviewers are, this is a formal, professional process, so adapt your behaviour accordingly.

Make sure you communicate equally with everyone on the panel; this is especially important when there is a service user or Expert by Experience on the panel. Check that everyone has understood you. If you do not understand what you are being asked in an interview, ask for clarification.

Be as professional as you can, even if you are very nervous or it is your first time applying for work. Remember this is a professional interaction. By the same token, if you happen to know your interviewers well or they are very friendly and chatty, do not forget that they will be scoring your performance against an agreed list of criteria and you need to remain as calm and professional as possible. You should adopt the same approach whether the post you are being interviewed for is paid or voluntary.

Practice your interview skills, including things like shaking hands and introducing yourself. Think about some questions you might want to ask the panel members at the end of an interview; it is likely that they will ask you if you have any questions and it is a valuable opportunity to ask something that will demonstrate you are interested and committed.

Do not pretend to know things you do not know; it is fine to say that you do not have experience or specific knowledge but try and show that you are keen to learn and to apply what you know from your education and life so far.

It is easy to say, but try not to be too upset and disappointed if you do not get the job; there is often a lot of competition and it is best to prepare to expect some setbacks. Do ask for feedback about what you might have done differently and express interest in hearing about any posts that might become available in the future. Thank your interviewers and demonstrate calm professionalism in the way you communicate, whether you are offered the post or not.

A newly qualified clinical psychologist advises: "*Find yourself a mentor whom you respect and trust who can offer you guidance. Know your strengths and limitations – be honest about what they are and work hard to develop them – you are not expected to be perfect!*"

Remember that "one size fits all" does not apply when it comes to the work experience of who gets onto training programmes. You can stand out when applying for clinical psychology training by having had very different life and work experiences. We have trained many people who have had other careers and spent their lives in many different ways before applying for training. Those that have come through very different routes often have much to contribute to the training programme and in their work as clinical psychologists.

What comes next?

You now know the educational requirements for clinical psychology training and different forms of work experience. Remember, whatever work experience you gain, make sure you describe it clearly in your application form, and when you have interviews, be able to describe what you gained from the experience and how it demonstrates that you are suitable to train as a clinical psychologist. The next chapter describes the process of applying for clinical psychology training.

4 Becoming a trainee

How do I train to be a clinical psychologist?

So far in this book we have described what a clinical psychologist is, the educational requirements for applying to become a clinical psychologist and the relevant work experience that it is important to get. If you are thinking that this is the career for you, and you have Graduate Basis for Chartered membership (GBC) of the British Psychological Society (BPS) (see Chapter 1), relevant work experience and/or have undertaken further postgraduate study, then the next step is to apply for a place on a clinical psychology training programme. This chapter describes how to do this and will be followed by a chapter on the basic structure of clinical psychology training to help you to prepare for what is ahead.

You will know by now that the competition for a place on clinical psychology training in the UK is fierce. As we have previously noted, of a total of 3866 applicants in 2018, only 593 secured a place to train – a 15% success rate. The majority of those 3866 applicants will have met the minimum essential entry criteria, will have undertaken relevant work experience, have a high 2:1 or a 1st for their first degree in psychology and many will have gained postgraduate degrees too. With a limited number of commissioned places on UK clinical psychology training programmes, there is a "bottle neck" at the application stage – too many strong applicants applying for a relatively small number of places. Successful applicants have almost always applied for at least a couple of previous years without success before they are offered a place. Although these statistics can be off-putting, it is worth remembering that the vast majority of people who begin their clinical training successfully qualify and go into employment as a clinical psychologist. Compared to other health care training programmes, the attrition rate (those that do not complete the course) from clinical psychology training is tiny. For example, in the academic year 2016–17, the attrition or drop-out rate was only 0.6%, which includes people who withdrew from a course and people who were unsuccessful in passing (data obtained from the Clearing House for Postgraduate Courses in Clinical Psychology – www.leeds.ac.uk/chpccp/numbers.html). Of those who completed their clinical training in 2017 and returned data to the Clearing House, 94.8% took up employment as a clinical psychologist or in an equivalent post, within 12 months of graduating. This is in line with the rate for the previous four years, which was between 93% and 97% each year. Of those working as clinical psychologists or at an equivalent level, 94.9% were working in the NHS or in other public sector funded posts (data obtained from the Clearing House for Postgraduate Courses in Clinical Psychology – www.leeds.ac.uk/chpccp/numbers.html).

If you have decided to pursue a career in clinical psychology, the application process will probably be the most difficult stage of the process; it is likely to be arduous and you will need to be prepared for rejection. Persistence, resilience and an ability to live with uncertainty are all qualities needed to be an effective clinical psychologist; the challenging path to securing a training place will help you to develop and demonstrate these qualities! Data on this and much more are available from the British Psychological Society's Alternative Handbook (https://shop.bps.org.uk/).

Applying for clinical psychology training in the UK

The most common way to apply for clinical psychology training in the UK is through the Clearing House for Postgraduate Courses in Clinical Psychology (www.leeds.ac.uk/chpccp/). The Clearing House website has a very helpful FAQs section (www.leeds.ac.uk/chpccp/faq.html). The Clearing House also provides a downloadable guide to the application process (www.leeds.ac.uk/chpccp/start.html).

Applying through the Clearing House for Postgraduate Courses in Clinical Psychology

There are 32 clinical psychology training programmes in the UK, and applications to 30 of these are administered through the Clearing House. The Clearing House website provides up to date, comprehensive information about applying for clinical psychology training in the UK, which includes detailed information about each of the 30, as well as information about funding, entry requirements and the application process itself. Applicants complete the application process online via the Clearing House website and may apply to up to four courses. In 2018, the processing fee charged by the Clearing House was £23, with a reduced early bird rate of £13.

What about the two programmes that operate differently and do not use the Clearing House?

There are two programmes that do not operate through the Clearing House – for information about the Doctorate in Clinical Psychology programme at Queen's University, Belfast, and the Clinical Psychology Doctorate at the University of Hull, you will need to consult the respective university websites.

Applications to the University of Hull's Doctorate in Clinical Psychology training programme can only be made via the "fast track" route offered to psychology undergraduates at the Universities of York and Hull.

Applications to the Doctorate in Clinical Psychology programme at Queen's University, Belfast, are made directly via the university.

Are all clinical psychology training programmes the same?

Whilst there is consistency across the 32 programmes insofar as they all need to meet the same standards set by the HCPC and the BPS, every clinical psychology programme does this slightly differently and has its own "flavour", and not every programme covers the same therapeutic approaches. Therefore, it is important that you check the details of each programme and that you understand what each programme offers before deciding where to apply.

How do I find out what the different training programmes are like?

You can do this by going onto the Clearing House for Postgraduate Courses in Clinical Psychology website (www.leeds.ac.uk/chpccp/) and reading about the 30 course centres that you can apply to via the Clearing House. In addition, more information about the programmes is available via their university websites. The British Psychological Society's Division of Clinical Psychology's Alternative Handbook for Postgraduate Training Courses in Clinical Psychology – https://shop.bps.org.uk/ – also provides an invaluable consumer view about every aspect of the programmes by collating responses from trainees who are actually studying on those programmes.

How are the clinical psychology training programmes funded?

The 32 UK clinical psychology training programmes are funded by the NHS. Most trainee clinical psychologists are salaried employees of the NHS on Band 6 (Agenda for Change – starting salary in 2018 was £28,050). The NHS also pays the university tuition fees. Trainee clinical psychologists are usually employed by a host NHS trust or board as full-time employees on a three-year fixed-term contract. They are also full-time registered postgraduate university students. A minority of UK programmes also offer self-funded places, and details of these can be found on the Clearing House website and on the university websites of the individual programmes.

As we discussed in Chapter 2 there has been uncertainty about the future funding of clinical psychology training in England since the government's Comprehensive Spending Review announcement in November 2015. This led to a decision by the UK government to end NHS funding in England for a number of health care programmes, including nursing, midwifery and the allied health professions – with funding shifting from Health Education England to the Student Loans system. For now, however and at the time this book went to print, clinical psychology training in England continues to be funded through the NHS (Health Education England), although this may be subject to change. Any information relating to changes in funding will be provided on the Clearing House website.

Are trainees employees or students?

They are usually both. As salaried employees of the NHS, trainees have contracts with the NHS and the terms and conditions of employment of all NHS staff as outlined under Agenda for Change. Trainees are also registered postgraduate students with the university that operates the training programme on which they are registered and, as such, have access to most of the benefits and opportunities that student status offers. It is worth checking out with an individual university what this might include in terms of financial, learning and academic support as well as any discounts and social and academic opportunities that are available.

Am I too young or too old to train?

There are no age restrictions to application for training. The majority of trainee clinical psychologists are in their late 20s when they begin their training. A sizeable minority are aged 30 years plus and a few train in their 40s or later. Respondents to the survey that forms the British Psychological Society's (BPS) Alternative Handbook give their ages so you can find the breakdown of age of trainees per programme in the handbook. Training later in life should not be viewed as a disadvantage;

in fact it can bring significant advantages to the individual trainee and the profession more widely.

What if I am a parent or have children whilst I am training?

Some trainees become parents during their training and as salaried employees of the NHS, trainees receive full parental benefits and rights – maternity leave, adoption leave and parental leave. The training programmes will work hard to make reasonable adjustments for trainees who have caring responsibilities for children or for other dependents.

> *Work/life balance was very difficult – I was a mother of two young children then and there were times when I found it difficult to meet the demands of the course and being a mother. I have found that by being organised, sticking to the routine and agenda of the day, and working in the evenings when they were in bed helped to free up time over the weekend for family time.*
>
> (Qualified clinical psychologist)

Can I train part-time?

At the time of writing all of the training programmes operate on a full-time basis (i.e. Monday to Friday). It is recognised that this might disadvantage some people from being able to apply to train and there are moves within the profession to try and develop part-time training routes, but as yet these are not established. Programmes do endeavour to make reasonable adjustments for trainees returning from parental leave or long-term sickness absence and flexible solutions can often be found to addressing trainees needs. At the moment, however, it is best to consider clinical psychology training to be a full-time occupation for the period of at least three years.

How many people apply?

Table 4.1 Number of Clearing House Applicants and Places per Course, 2012–18

Year	*Applicants*	*Places*	*Success Rate*
2018	3866	593	15%
2017	3932	594	15%
2016	3730	595	16%
2015	3698	591	16%
2014	3796	583	15%
2013	3725	594	16%
2012	3857	586	15%

Source: Clearing House for Postgraduate Courses in Clinical Psychology (www.leeds.ac.uk/chpccp/)

What is the time frame for applying?

Whilst the timeline for applications will vary a little from year to year (check the Clearing House website to find the exact dates for the year within which you intend to apply), the general timeline is:

- Applications open in September.
- Closing date for applications is the end of November (with a discounted "early bird" rate).
- Applications are released by the Clearing House to all course centres between the beginning of December and the end of January.
- Courses will screen and shortlist the applications, once they are received from the Clearing House, between the beginning of December and the end of February.
- Preselection/screening tests (where applicable) are held between February and mid-March.
- Course centres inform applicants if they have been shortlisted or not by mid-March.
- Interviews are held between mid-March and the end of May.

- Course centres inform all interviewees of the results of their interviews by the beginning of June and applicants must respond to all offers shortly afterwards.

When do training programmes start?

Although the exact start date for each of the programmes varies, all courses start between early September and mid-October and have only one intake per academic year.

See Clearing House site for information for international students.

Which factors should I consider when choosing which programmes to apply to?

Applicants can apply for up to four course centres in each application round. Decisions about which programmes to apply for are made on the basis of a range of factors. Applicants are often guided by geographical preferences and may be attracted to study at particular universities. Other factors that affect the decision about where to apply to might include the impression they have of the programme staff and trainees given in the Alternative Handbook; differences in selection processes and course content; the number of places available; evidence of meaningful involvement of Experts by Experience in the programme; the programme's values and underpinning philosophy; the types of assessment methods (written exams as opposed to no written exams, for example); the type of placement locations, specialist placements available and so on. Some courses may offer accreditation in specific psychological therapy models (such as cognitive behaviour therapy or systemic therapy) although all courses are required to include training in CBT and at least one other evidence-based psychological therapy.

Do I need to be able to drive?

As we describe in the next chapter, trainees complete a range of work placements over their three years of training. Almost all programmes use placements over a wide geographical area to accommodate all their trainees' needs, so trainees know that they are likely to be required to travel some distance for at least some of their placements. Some clinical psychology training programmes require all applicants to have a driver's licence unless there is a reason why they are unable to drive (e.g. because of disability).

How big are the programmes?

You may wish to consider the number of trainees in each cohort when deciding which programmes might suit you. At the time of writing, the number of places on clinical psychology training programmes in the UK is determined by NHS education and training commissioners. The smallest programmes have 10 training places in each year whilst the largest has 42 in each year. As mentioned earlier in this chapter, the BPS's Alternative Handbook is a good place to look for details on variation between courses on these, and other, factors.

If you have more than one interview for training, we advise that you use the experience of attending the interviews to gain an understanding of each particular programme and to decide which you prefer should you be in the happy position of having more than one offer of a place.

Completing the Clearing House application form

The application form asks for a range of details – see the Clearing House website for details. Course centres use the application form for the initial stage of shortlisting to screen out any applications that do not meet the essential minimum criteria. Some then go on to use screening tests to shortlist applicants for interview. Some shortlist from the application forms but then do not use them in the interview process.

Top tips for completing your application form

- Leave plenty of time to write your application form, as you are likely to have a lot of material that you want to include. You are likely to need to edit this so that it comes within the maximum word limit for each section of the form.

- Check the minimum entry requirements for the programmes you are applying for and ensure that you meet them before going ahead with your application.
- Read the Clearing House entries and university website for the programmes you are applying to so that you know what their selection criteria are and can demonstrate how you meet these on your application form.
- Ask trainees, clinical psychologists and others that know you to read through your draft application form. Consider asking service users and carers for feedback on your qualities too.
- Make sure that you complete the application form accurately and that it is free from typos and spelling and grammatical errors. Proofread it carefully and, if possible, ask someone else to proofread it too. It gives a really poor impression if your application form is not completed professionally.
- Write concisely – being able to communicate clearly and succinctly is important for the job. Your application form is a chance to demonstrate this ability.
- Use the application form to demonstrate what you have learned from your experience so far. "*Try to reflect on your experience rather than listing everything you have done on your application*" (Year 1 trainee). "*It is sometimes less about your experience and more about what you have learnt from it*" (Recently qualified clinical psychologist).
- Clinical psychology training courses encourage applications from those who have experience of emotional distress/using mental health services/psychological therapy. If you feel comfortable mentioning your own experience, courses will welcome this, but it is by no means compulsory.
- If this is relevant for you, it might be helpful to reflect on why these experiences have influenced your career choice and talk about this at your interview. Demonstrate how these experiences have shaped your wish to train as a clinical psychologist and how this will positively inform your training and clinical practice.
- Take care to convey yourself as a rounded person on the application form. Remember that people who are shortlisting a whole batch of application forms only have your form and the two references to look at; they do not know you. Ensure that the strongest aspects of

your experience or attributes make you stand out from the crowd and make your application memorable. However, it is best to avoid jokes or saying things to try and shock the reader.

- Demonstrate that you have a life and interests outside of psychology/clinical psychology. Write about these and what attributes they illustrate about you as a person and your suitability to be a clinical psychologist.
- Do the thinking for the people rating your application form. For example, if you had a gap year and travelled around the world, explain how this demonstrates that you are resilient, how it shows that you cope well with uncertainty, that it helped to feed your curiosity about people etc. Simply stating it as a fact misses an opportunity to expand on yourself and your attributes.
- Show that you are self-aware. "*Know yourself, you're going to need you! You are the biggest strategy for your clients' therapy and future psychological well-being*" (Recently qualified clinical psychologist).
- Show that you are aware that there are strengths and limitations of the profession of clinical psychology: "*Speak to people that have had bad experiences of therapy . . . you'll learn a lot*" (Recently qualified clinical psychologist).

Referees

Applicants are required to provide details of two people who will act as their referees; one is an "academic" referee and the other a "relevant experience" referee. Choosing your referees and ensuring that they understand what is required by courses is an important, but sometimes overlooked, part of the process.

It is essential to choose your referees wisely. You should ensure that the two referees meet the Clearing House's requirements – details about what is required from each referee are provided on the Clearing House's website. Make sure that you approach potential referees and ask them whether they will be able to provide you with a reference and whether you can put their contact details on your application form.

Some applicants are disadvantaged by using referees who give very minimal information for shortlisters to assess. It can be a real obstacle to getting shortlisted for an interview if your referees do not know you well, don't know what clinical psychology training involves or cannot give evidence of the skills and qualities that make you a good candidate for training.

Make sure your referees know you

The "academic" referee must be able to comment on your academic ability and preferably have direct experience of your academic work. In particular, they need to be able to comment on the standard of your academic work in the context of considering your suitability for postgraduate doctoral level studies. Often a dissertation supervisor will make a good referee, as they will usually have worked more closely with you than lecturers and will know your research and academic writing abilities well. If your "academic" referee is someone you have not had contact with for several years, then make sure that they know what you have been doing since you completed your course with them so that they have some context and can include this in their reference. If your interest in clinical psychology was clear when you were at university, then it would be beneficial if your referee could mention this. If this was not the case, your referee could mention what you have been doing since you graduated and how this has helped to shape your interest in clinical psychology and prepare you for training.

The "experience" referee must be able to comment on your performance in a relevant clinical and/or research context. Where possible, this person should be your current employer.

Make sure your referees know about clinical psychology training

It is very helpful for referees to be reminded of the information that they might need to include in their reference for you and to make sure that they know what a clinical psychology training programme is looking for so they can write their reference accordingly. Some referees write many clinical psychology references and are well practiced at it. If the person you have chosen has not written such references before, you would be well advised to help them understand what clinical psychology training is and what attributes a shortlister might be looking for in a reference. Our advice would be, if at all possible use a referee who knows what clinical psychology training entails and can link your attributes to the requirements of training.

Applicants with disabilities

All of the course centres welcome applications from people with disabilities. Full details can be found at www.leeds.ac.uk/chpccp/disability.html. Some employers operate the Disability Confident scheme (which was previously known as the "two ticks" or "double-tick" scheme). This is a voluntary scheme that organisations can choose to sign up to. It aims to help organisations make the most of the opportunities provided by employing disabled people. Information about this can be found at www.gov.uk/government/collections/disability-confident-campaign.

People who have all sorts of disabilities and differences train to become clinical psychologists and the profession benefits from their additional insights. Universities have specialist guidance and support services for students with a range of disabilities and support needs and these are available for trainees. The services they offer will include confidential one-to-one appointments; assistance with obtaining funding to support disability-related study needs such as the Disabled Students' Allowance; identification of individual reasonable adjustments; loan of specialist equipment and software; liaison with academic and other university departments to communicate and implement reasonable adjustments; provision of study assistants such as note takers or proofreaders.

A Deaf clinical psychologist, who has been qualified for five years, recalls her experience of training:

> *As I am Deaf and communicate using British Sign Language, I am not seen as a "conventional" clinical psychologist (either as a trainee or qualified). The biggest challenge I faced whilst undergoing training was linked to being Deaf. Many of my supervisors had initial concerns in how clients would react to me – especially for those who were non-Deaf/hearing. They also had some concerns in how I would undertake therapy using sign language interpreters. These were unfounded, as over time my supervisors realised that I was able to conduct my*

role effectively and being Deaf as well as having interpreters did not affect therapy with my clients. What I found really useful was having the same team of interpreters (I had four interpreters) and used the same interpreter when undergoing therapy with my client to help with consistency. Also I disregarded Deaf culture in the initial sessions to enable to reduce client's anxiety and to improve engagement. I found this difficult initially when they looked away from me and looked at the interpreter but by the third session they did look at me. Also I had to reduce my facial expression as I was frightening the clients (!) (Deaf people use facial expression instead of tone of voice to demonstrate the severity of the action such as slightly anxious to extremely anxious).

Another challenge I had was the Disabled Student Allowance (DSA) which would pay for interpreters and note takers (I was unable to take notes whilst watching the interpreters). The money from the DSA only covered several weeks in the first year [of training] which gave me a lot of anxiety whether I would be able to continue. The university was excellent and they also spent a lot of time and effort in sourcing extra funding and this was found one day prior to DSA running out! If you get a place at university, apply for DSA immediately and also to inform the team if there is a shortfall and that they need to source additional funding from elsewhere.

As NHS employees, trainees also have access to support from their employing Trust, and some forms of support and reasonable adjustments may be provided by the NHS. Training programmes have successfully supported trainees who have a wide range of physical and learning support needs so do not assume that any support needs you might have would preclude you from training.

Diversity, inclusivity and equal opportunities

The Clearing House provides a detailed breakdown of equal opportunities data for every year of applications. See www.leeds.ac.uk/chpccp/.

The profession of clinical psychology in the UK remains a relatively non-diverse group, which is a significant cause for concern. Much has been written about the lack of ethnic diversity and the low number of men coming in to the profession, as well as lack of diversity on other dimensions such as social class and education. See, for example, Turpin and Coleman (2010). Recent data makes the case for clinical psychology trainers in the UK, and others involved in education, to urgently address the lack of diversity in the profession.

The BPS's Minorities in Clinical Training Group is working to address the need for equality and diversity in the profession, playing a crucial role in awareness raising and actively campaigning for change. For more details, go to https://www.bps.org.uk/member-microsites/division-clinical-psychology/dcpgroups.

We recommend reading more about the experience of being a trainee clinical psychologist from a black and minority ethnic group in a study carried out by Shah, Wood, Nolte and Goodbody (2012).

A male Year 2 trainee clinical psychologist reflects:

> *It is also useful to acknowledge that the discipline is female heavy which is interesting in itself. This can have implications on teaching, as responses seem to frequently come from a female perspective or male trainees may feel reluctant to voice their opinions in fear of offending others. There have also been occasions where I am the only male staff member in a team. Similarly, there is little ethnic diversity across the discipline, so again these may exacerbate opportunities where an individual can feel particularly exposed, vulnerable or unsure. However, I have found peers and clinicians appreciate an alternative perspective should such trainees feel brave enough to speak up.*

Navigating the process: advice from current trainees

We asked for some reflections and advice on applying for training from people who have been through it:

- *I wish I had known that a lot of getting on training is not all about your experience (although of course this is important). It is also about what you have gained from it, what sort of person you are and what your personal values are. At first I thought it was all about getting lots of experience and academic qualifications, but it's also very much a personal journey of reflection and self-awareness.*

  (Trainee)

- *Get published – can you publish your undergraduate thesis, or expand on this afterwards for publication? I carried on doing research with my undergrad supervisor to get a publication.*

  (Year 3 trainee clinical psychologist)

- *Reflect on your values, what is important to you (in your work and outside of work). Reflect on your practice/experiences as you go along as much as you can. Don't just gain experience – learn from experience. Read (books, papers, The Psychologist, news articles). Be aware of current issues facing the NHS, clinical psychology and in the world more generally.*

  (Year 2 trainee clinical psychologist)

Preselection tests

Some courses use computerised or written tests as part of their shortlisting process and these are usually held from January to mid-March. These may include an online general mental ability test with verbal and numerical reasoning elements. Others require applicants who pass their initial minimum criteria screening to sit a multiple choice test.

More information about courses that use preselection tests as part of their selection procedures can be found on the Clearing House website. Make sure that you are available to take tests and interviews during the stated time frames.

Interviews

Each course has its own interview process. Details of what to expect are included in the course centre entries on the Clearing House website/university websites. Most selection procedures for clinical psychology training involve one or two panel interviews. The panel will usually consist of a mixture of programme staff/academics, NHS clinical psychologists and EbEs involved with the course. Some programmes also employ an interview task as part of the process. These may include giving a presentation, involvement in a group or individual task with service users, role plays or a discussion of a video excerpt. Whilst the interview processes will vary from programme to programme, in general all interviews will cover academic/research experience/competence and clinical experience.

Top tips for a successful interview

- If possible, practise your interview technique by doing some mock interviews. This will help you to practise coping with feeling nervous and allow you to get feedback on how you come across in a formal interview situation. Have a think about the types of questions that you may be asked, and practise answering them. Read about the course you are being interviewed for on the course university website and the Clearing House course centre entry. Being able to think on your feet is important as a clinical psychologist, and programmes want you to demonstrate this ability during the interview process.
- Remember that the interviewers know that most candidates will feel nervous about being interviewed. They will be looking for a candidate's ability to gain mastery over their nervousness and to perform well in the interview despite how they are feeling. Achieving this is possible but takes practice. Remember, there are plenty of aspects of clinical training and the work of a clinical psychologist that make us feel anxious; the skill is being able to manage these feelings safely and professionally so that you can still cope and do the job well. The interview is an opportunity to demonstrate this ability.
- Familiarise yourself with the current NHS policy context and relevant political context and be prepared to talk about these issues in the interview.
- Be prepared for interview questions that require a degree of self-disclosure and an ability to demonstrate your capacity for appropriate levels of disclosure and self-reflection.
- Do not over-prepare answers and sound rehearsed or like a textbook.
- Make sure you know as much as possible about the programme you are being interviewed for and can say something about why that particular programme/university/geographical locality appeals to you.
- If you have had a different career and have decided to change and become a clinical psychologist, then prepare to talk about how your

previous experience demonstrates some of the skills and aptitudes needed to be a clinical psychologist. We have known nurses, solicitors, police officers, bankers, social workers, actors and many others successfully train and qualify as clinical psychologists. This is also true for those who have come to training later because they have been bringing up a family, had other carer commitments or have been having other life experiences. Coming into the profession from a range of different life experiences and/or careers is often beneficial and enriches the profession, helping it become more diverse: showcase this at the interview. A Year 1 trainee reflects on the fact that he had little experience of clinical psychology when he applied to do clinical psychology training: "*It's cool to come into clinical psychology from outside of the usual routes. Initially, it felt daunting on the clinical psychology training programme as my main background was not in clinical psychology or psychology more broadly. However, this background has really helped. It particularly gives me respect for other professionals – especially psychiatry*".

- The 32 programmes are all slightly different (see earlier in this chapter) – be aware of this. Remember that you are looking for the programme that best suits you.
- Do not be too strongly influenced by what you read online or on forums. These can be useful sources of support and helpful when finding out about the different programmes, but remember how easily myths and rumours can appear to be fact when written online. Every year there are "facts" that go around about the interviews for the different programmes and "facts" about what the programmes are like that bear no resemblance to the reality. The best way to find out about a programme is to talk to the trainees who are actually on it and look at the BPS's Alternative Handbook.

Dealing with rejection – if at first you don't succeed . . .

When you have a strong application go ahead and apply for training, but be prepared for rejection and remember that this is an almost inevitable part of the process. Contrary to often-cited opinion, the process of application for clinical psychology training is not a lottery, but it is a highly competitive process being undertaken by a great many excellent candidates.

Rejection never feels good and it's likely you will have made a huge investment of time, energy and emotion into applying for training, which can make rejection feel particularly hard to manage.

Tips to consider if you have been rejected

- Remember that you are in good company – most people who become clinical psychologists will have had the experience of not getting offers of interviews or not being offered a training place after interview. In 2017 the average (mean) age of those starting training was 28 years, although, because the distribution is skewed, this could be slightly misleading. In fact, the most frequent starting age was 26 and nearly a third were aged 25 or under.
- The more experience you get prior to getting in a course, the better equipped you will be to do the training.
- Get as much feedback as you can about where you could have earned more points – this might help you decide whether there are things you can do differently. For example, get some different work experience, choose a different referee and try to get involved in research.

  > *The ups and downs of the road to training are not indicative of your worth, rather they are indicative of the process. There can also be skills that you need to acquire but when you find this out it can be helpful to think 'this tells me I need to learn x' rather than 'I did terribly'. Focusing on what you need to do rather than taking it as a judgement on yourself can be a helpful way to get the strength to keep moving forward.*
  >
  > (Year 1 trainee clinical psychologist)

  It is a good idea to keep copies of your application form and any notes you made after the interview; these can help you prepare for next time.
- Talk to the people who helped you prepare as well as those who interviewed you. If you did not get any help or support with your

application or interview technique think about doing so before your next applications.

- Take a break from thinking about it for a while.
- If you are in a lot of contact with other people who are also applying, think about how much contact you want to have when they are getting their offers/rejections. Remember that clinical psychology is a small world and it is important to be professional in the way you respond to other people's news no matter what you might privately feel about it.
- Seek support from friends and others who can talk through how you are feeling and help you consider your next steps.

How many times should I try to get on a course?

It depends on why you are not being successful. Remember that people often apply for clinical psychology training a number of times. Bear in mind that most people are not successful the first time they apply. Based on the 2019 BPS Alternative Handbook, the majority of new starters to training had applied unsuccessfully once or twice previously, although only a small percentage gained a training place after four or more attempts.

If you know that your application is not yet strong enough because you do not have enough relevant experience then we would urge you not to give up, but to focus on your work and strengthen your application for another year. The programmes do not keep a log of how many times people apply and no one receives extra points or sanctions for applying multiple times.

If you are not being successful for a reason relating to your references or the way you present yourself at interview, consider whether this is a factor that you can do something about (e.g. learn better interview technique) or if it is an indication that you are just not suited to the profession (e.g. you seem to have fixed ideas or prejudices about people). This will help you decide whether to continue to try or to change direction. There are many careers outside clinical psychology, and feedback of this type might help you decide that you would be better suited to something else. Of course, another reason for being unsuccessful is that, although you would make a perfectly good clinical psychologist, competition for places is so high that not everyone who is suitable can get on.

A Year 2 trainee clinical psychologist reflects:

> *It is important to remember that there is more to life than CP training! I struggled to notice this in the early years after completing my undergraduate as I was keen to feel like I was moving in the right direction. I feel I was more successful with applications/interviews once I had accepted that clinical psychology training was not the be all and end all of my professional development/career.*

A Year 3 trainee clinical psychologist:

> *You need to be resilient, hard-working, and persevere but always have a plan B. If you seem desperate to get on the course and it is your only focus in life, that may not be a good thing.*

Some people decide that after several rounds of rejections, they are no longer going to pursue clinical psychology as a career path. There is no right or wrong time to make that decision but it is always worth asking yourself:

- Are you are getting rejections because clinical psychology is simply not a good fit for you?
- Are there other professions that would make use of your skills and interests?
- Can you financially afford to continue to keep applying?

What comes next?

In this chapter we have covered the process of applying for training as a clinical psychologist. We have discussed why this can be the most difficult stage of becoming a clinical psychologist. We hope that some of the advice and hints from trainees and people who have been through it will have been helpful. In the next chapter we describe what clinical psychology training is actually like.

5 Being a trainee

In Chapter 4 we described the process of applying for clinical psychology training from application to interview. Gaining a place on a training programme is often the most difficult stage of becoming a clinical psychologist, so it is important to know whether it will be worth all the time and effort. To help, this chapter briefly describes the main components of a clinical psychology training programme in the UK; how trainees spend their time; how their progress and competence is measured; the best and most challenging aspects of training, and reflections and advice from past and current trainees. We hope this will help you consider whether you would be suited to undertaking training to become a clinical psychologist yourself.

How long does it take to train to be a clinical psychologist and what degree do you get at the end?

In the UK, clinical psychology training programmes usually take three years of full-time study to complete. If you are successful, you will be awarded a doctorate in clinical psychology. This entitles you to call yourself a Doctor of Clinical Psychology and, in the UK, to register with the Health and Care Professions Council (HCPC). This is a mandatory requirement on successful completion of training and entitles you to use the job title "clinical psychologist". Clinical psychologist is one of the protected titles under the HCPC which means that only people who are registered with the HCPC are permitted to use it – see the later section on the HCPC for more detail.

Do all clinical psychologists have a doctorate in clinical psychology?

No – in the UK the move to make training a doctoral-level qualification took place in the early 1990s. Clinical psychologists who trained before then may not have a doctorate in clinical psychology but have an MSc in clinical psychology or a British Psychological Society diploma in clinical psychology instead. Their training and the jobs they do, however, are the same. Likewise, clinical psychologists with Master's level qualifications who trained outside the UK may be able to register with the HCPC and practise in the UK if they are able to demonstrate that they meet all of the standards of proficiency.

As the knowledge and skills base of the profession has continued to develop, so have the training programmes. Although clinical psychologists who trained some years ago will have spent their time in lectures and on placements in the NHS like current trainees, some of the learning and teaching methods have changed considerably over time. The development of new therapeutic approaches means that some aspects of the curriculum for present-day trainees are different to those studied by their more experienced colleagues. This is akin to how medicine is always developing and doctors who train now are learning different content and in different ways to those who trained in the past. Part of the joy of working as a clinical psychologist is that the evidence base about psychological distress and the approaches that are helpful develop continually and thus one never stops having to learn new things, even when qualified for many years.

Who regulates clinical psychology training?

All of the UK clinical psychology training programmes are postgraduate and at doctoral level. Each programme must be approved by the HCPC and accredited by the British Psychological Society (BPS).

The HCPC regulates 16 health and care professions, including clinical psychologists. In order to call yourself a clinical psychologist and practise in the UK, it is a legal requirement to be registered with the HCPC. The HCPC approves the education and training programmes that lead to access to registration and the HCPC has to ensure that clinical psychology programmes are training people to be clinical psychologists to their required standards.

What is the role of the British Psychological Society (BPS)?

The BPS is the representative body for psychology and psychologists in the UK. It is responsible for promoting "excellence and ethical practice in the science, education and practical applications of the discipline" (http://bps.org.uk/about-us). One of the BPS's responsibilities is the accreditation of educational programmes, including UK clinical psychology training. Accreditation through partnership is the process by which the BPS works with education providers to ensure that quality standards in education and training are met by all courses and training programmes on an ongoing basis.

Experts by Experience: involvement in clinical psychology training

The HCPC and BPS both require clinical psychology training programmes to work with service users and carers (often referred to as Experts by Experience, or EbEs) in the delivery of the programmes. The extent to which this is the case varies across programmes and may be a factor you wish to consider when deciding which programmes to apply for. Many programmes include EbEs in their selection and interview processes and all will involve EbEs to a greater or lesser degree in teaching as lecturers and as peer reviewers. Experts by Experience will also play a role in research and evaluation on some programmes and as co-supervisors and/or mentors to trainees on placement. Some programmes have EbE groups working as an integral part of the programme structure and co-producing much of the programme, and a small number have an EbE member of staff as part of the programme team. Whatever their roles, EbEs have a crucial voice in defining what makes a good clinical psychologist (which we discussed in Chapter 2) and how best training can accomplish this.

A recently qualified clinical psychologist recalls that one of the best aspects of training was the opportunity to hear "*hundreds of highly experienced clinicians and service users impart their knowledge and experience*", highlighting the impact of being taught not just by clinical psychologists but by those who identify as service users and carers.

What do trainee clinical psychologists do?

In this section we briefly describe the main activities undertaken by trainees: clinical placements, attending university for teaching/lectures, research and coursework/exams.

What trainees do: clinical placements

Trainees spend approximately 50% of their three-year training gaining direct clinical experience through work placements in a range of services. In order to meet the HCPC and BPS standards, all trainees have to develop competencies in working with people across the life span (children and teenagers, adults of working age and older adults) as well as with people presenting a range of different psychological difficulties and conditions, abilities and disabilities and with a variety of communication needs. This means that most trainees will complete five or six placements during their training that range in length from six months to a year. Trainees have to undertake core placements, or gain core placement experiences, in work with adults of working age in mental health services, older adults/people with chronic health/neuropsychological issues, people with intellectual disabilities (also referred to as learning disabilities) and with children and adolescents. There are also opportunities to undertake specialist or elective placements, usually in the third year of training. When looking at the different programmes, you may wish to check which specialist placements are available, as these vary depending on the services in the local geographical area. Placements usually take place alongside time in teaching, hence the week may consist of three days a week on placement and two days in teaching, though the balance will change across the three years and each course's timetable looks a little different.

Trainees work in a range of settings during their training. These are usually in NHS/social care services but sometimes in the third sector – that is, non-governmental and non-profit-making organisations or associations including charities, voluntary and community groups, cooperatives, etc. Placements may be based in community multidisciplinary teams working alongside nurses, support workers, psychiatrists, social workers, occupational therapists, speech and language therapists, doctors, physiotherapists and other psychological therapists. Other placements are situated in hospitals working on wards, in-patient units and secure units, and in a whole range of out-patient clinic and community settings.

> *It was great being able to have placements in up to six different clinical areas. There are such a diverse range of places that clinical psychologists work, which means that placements are very different to each other.*
>
> (Year 1 trainee)

All trainees have at least one clinical psychologist supervisor for the duration of every placement. The quality of the placement is monitored by the training programme staff, and at least one visit to the placement to review the trainee's progress takes place for every placement.

The length of placements varies. It is common for core placements to be for six months and Year 3 specialist or elective placements to be 6 to 12 months long, but programmes do vary somewhat.

Whilst on placement, trainees complete a range of work, depending on the client group, the setting and their stage of training and needs. Ways of working will include:

- Individual psychological assessment and therapy.
- Working indirectly with service users through family members or paid staff.
- Group work – including group therapy and psychoeducational groups.
- Consultation.
- Delivering training.
- Service evaluation/development.

Whilst every trainee must meet the required standards of the programme, each trainee's clinical experience will be unique. Trainees are required to keep an individual log or portfolio of their clinical skills development and professional competencies throughout the three years. This provides a record of their competencies as they are achieved, enables them to record their therapeutic competencies in the different models they learn (cognitive behaviour therapy, plus at least one other psychological therapy model) and ensures that they are benchmarked against recognised accredited competency frameworks.

Geographical areas in the UK differ and courses based in rural areas may use placements over a very large geographical area. Even city-based training programmes use placements in services that may be considerable distances from the university base, so trainees know that they are likely to be required to travel some distance for at least some of their placements. Some clinical psychology training programmes require all applicants to the programme to have a driver's licence unless there is a reason why they are unable to drive (e.g. because of disability).

What trainees do: teaching

Trainees are required to attend teaching at their university for a significant proportion of their time – usually one to two days per week in term time. Some programmes provide teaching that maps onto the clinical placements being undertaken at any point in time. For other programmes this is not feasible, so trainees may be doing a placement in one clinical area (e.g. children and young people) whilst receiving formal teaching on a different area altogether (e.g. older adults). Teaching will be provided by programme staff and other academic staff within the university, Experts by Experience and by NHS clinical psychologists and other professionals. Teaching formats will be varied on every programme and will include lectures, practical skills-based workshops, seminars, role plays and enquiry-based learning group work and presentations.

> *It's one of the best things about training – getting taught by such a range of experts – people who really know the job and do it for real – it can be very inspiring and gives you confidence to go and try what you*

have learned. It's really good when you get the chance to practise skills in the safety of the classroom before going on placement.

(Year 3 trainee)

What trainees do: research

You will have gathered that one of the central aspects of being a clinical psychologist relates to the ability to understand, use and undertake research. The skills to do this are taught on the programmes, and trainees have to demonstrate their abilities in a number of ways. They are required to carry out and write a report for a small-scale service evaluation/small-scale research project and also to carry out a larger and longer piece of research which forms the doctoral thesis submitted during the third year of training. Trainees are encouraged to start planning their doctoral research early on in the first year of training. Depending on the programme, trainees may pursue their own research ideas or may undertake a piece of research aligned to the research interests of university staff. Trainees are usually allocated two research supervisors (often, but not always, one academic and one clinician working in the area) and receive training in research methods and related research activity as part of the curriculum.

I found the research element rather challenging as it had never been one of my strengths or main interests. It was difficult to get to grips with the standard of research procedure and writing expected at a doctoral level. However, looking back at the process I realise the feedback I received was invaluable and now that I am qualified, I feel more open and able to get involved in future research.

(Newly qualified clinical psychologist)

What trainees do: coursework assignments/exams

All clinical psychology training programmes require trainees to complete coursework assignments, but the nature of these varies between different programmes. For example, some programmes have written examinations, while others do not. If this is an important factor for you, check it out when looking at the different programmes on offer. Types of coursework assignments include essays, case studies, enquiry based learning assessments, presentations, written examinations, assessed group work and submission of recorded placement work. Trainees' practice is also assessed on placement where their work will be observed and often recorded by their supervisors who have to assess and give feedback as part of ongoing learning and also as evidence for the trainee to pass the placement.

> *Recording your clinical sessions is one of the scariest but most helpful things you have to do as a trainee – once you get over how exposed you feel it's just the best learning tool!*
>
> (Year 3 trainee)

What trainees do: other exciting things . . .

Many trainees get involved in a whole range of other activities whilst they are on the training programme. This might include teaching or providing training to others, speaking at conferences, getting involved in widening participation events to teach other people about psychology, working with Experts by Experience, acting as buddies and mentors to other students, engaging in reflective practice and supervision groups . . . and more.

> *No two days are the same – it can feel like you are always at the edge of what you can manage but it's really exciting too.*
>
> (Year 3 trainee)

What support is available to trainees?

Training to be a clinical psychologist is not for the faint-hearted. It is a challenging and demanding three years of constant change, learning and assessment and a wide range of clinical and academic work. Many trainees talk about the experience of having to "keep many plates spinning" and the pressures associated with this.

> *The academic rigours were understandably difficult, especially as I had been out of an academic environment for some time before*

> *training. This can range from sitting and maintaining focus in lectures to meeting deadlines and understanding the expectations of writing reports/assignments at doctoral level. It can also feel difficult to manage a work-life balance; where inevitably there will be higher pressures with academic deadlines which can impact on personal life and vice versa. This can take some juggling to begin with, especially if you have chosen to relocate for training. Similarly, it can feel quite isolating if you have moved away, as postgrad, university experience is very different from undergraduate level and people already have relatively stable social groups which they might be protective of changing. The clinical placements can be challenging in themselves as it can feel that you are left to manage complex cases with very limited experience or knowledge. Being mindful that you have the necessary global therapeutic skills and using supervision effectively can mitigate this to some extent but you can regularly feel out of your depth which can take time to tolerate.*
>
> (Year 2 trainee)

All programmes recognise that training to be a clinical psychologist can be a challenge. It requires trainees to be good at multi-tasking; juggling being on placement with going to university for teaching and also completing coursework assignments and doctoral level research – all at the same time as maintaining a life outside work and training.

> *Be prepared for a lot of work, and I mean a lot! Very important to keep on top of it, and catch up if you get behind.*
>
> (Recently qualified clinical psychologist)

In addition, much can happen in a person's life during three years and sometimes adverse life events impact on training. Programme staff recognise these challenges and are required to provide a range of supports. Typically, these will include every trainee being allocated a personal tutor and/or academic advisor for the duration of their training. Most programmes also operate a buddy system, linking new trainees with a buddy into the year above. Programmes often operate mentor systems with NHS clinical psychologists. In addition, trainees are entitled to access the range of supports offered by universities to all students and, likewise, by NHS Trusts for all employees. These often include staff support and counselling services, occupational health and employee well-being and a range of academic support.

> *I feel very privileged to be a trainee, and I have found it a tough but very rewarding job. We have a lovely cohort so being a trainee has meant I have had the opportunity to meet lots of kind and similar-minded friends. I have also had some excellent supervisors on placement who have taken the time to nurture my skills while protecting me from the inevitable pressures of the NHS. I have also felt listened to and supported, my personal tutor particularly makes me feel that she wants me to do well.*
>
> (Year 1 trainee)

Trainees often report that one of the most powerful sources of support comes from other trainees.

> *The trainees on the course were fabulous and very supportive with me; I am still in touch with many of them. I learnt so much on the course (it can be overwhelming at times) with a fantastic array of tutors and visiting tutors.*
>
> (Recently qualified clinical psychologist)

> *The best part is ultimately there will be somebody on that training who will feel very similarly to you and you will feel like they get you so the bonds that you make with your peers during training will help you get through.*
>
> (Newly qualified clinical psychologist)

> *I loved training – some of it was hard and I failed some pieces of work but my cohort was brilliant – I made lifelong friends. It was tough but not insurmountable and I was pushed to the limit of what is reasonable to expect.*
>
> (Qualified clinical psychologist)

What's it like being a trainee?

We asked current trainee clinical psychologists and qualified clinical psychologists to tell us what they have found to be the best and most challenging aspects of being a trainee. You will notice themes about the variety of the roles that a trainee has to take on, the impact of training on one's self and more practical considerations.

> *I'm really enjoying my time as a trainee. It's busy, diverse and rewarding. There's a great mix of teaching time, placement time and personal study time. I had lots of "wobbles" prior to starting training (e.g. Am I doing the right thing? Am I good enough? Am I capable of studying at doctorate level?) but I can honestly say I am thoroughly enjoying it and haven't looked back once!*
>
> (Year 1 trainee)

> *Training is stressful, exciting, rewarding, not necessarily in that order! There are highs and lows, as you would expect. Generally, placements are brilliant and you get a real breadth of experience. Teaching is also generally great. Every time I feel it gets too much, I remind myself that I have the best job in the world and most days look forward to going to work – not many people can say that.*
>
> (Year 3 trainee)

> *It's absolutely fantastic – I love it. It's hard at times and there's always a challenge to face. However, the experiences I have gained: of meeting and working with all the people I have (the clients, the families, the supervisors, the tutors, the staff teams, the trainees), the learning I have gained through placement, training and such varied and thorough teaching, the thinking that is stimulated, the opportunities I've been given and the chance to pursue a career I feel so passionate about far outweigh the challenges. I feel very lucky to be in clinical training.*
>
> (Year 2 trainee)

> *Training can send you a bit mad if you actually allow yourself to engage fully, you have to engage with your own self, your history and what has made you. It's time-management hard. If you really do it you will come out of training changed and will continue to change throughout your working life – not all jobs do that. You can become a better person and can better use yourself in the service of others.*
>
> (Qualified clinical psychologist)

What are the best things about being a trainee?

We asked trainees and qualified clinical psychologists to tell us about the most positive and rewarding aspects of being a trainee and the most common themes related to the variety of the roles and the opportunities that the training makes available.

> *Being in a position where you can engage in further education and training while being employed as a clinical practitioner. I think this makes the job unique and I often think it is such a privilege to be given an opportunity to learn and develop knowledge as you become more confident clinically.*
>
> (Year 1 trainee)

> *It is comforting to know that you have a certain level of job security for a number of years.*
>
> (Year 2 trainee)

> *The privilege of working with such a diverse range of people who allow you into their lives in order to try to help them, the vast experience we gain (of different client groups, therapies and models, working with clinical psychologists) studying alongside a group of like-minded but unique trainee clinical psychologists, being part of a caring culture: striving to find ways to help people in the best ways we can.*
>
> (Year 2 trainee)

> *The best part of clinical training was the opportunity to vastly accelerate my clinical knowledge and skills. Though the fast pace of placements, teaching and assignments take some time to adjust to, my confidence and competence dramatically improved once I felt I had got into the flow of the programme. Additionally, being part of the training opens you to a close-knit community of likeminded mental health professionals and service users that I feel very privileged to be a part of.*
>
> (Newly qualified clinical psychologist)

What are the most challenging aspects of being a trainee?

Whilst the variety and breadth of the roles expected of trainees were often seen as positive, the accompanying demands tend to be reported when trainees talk about the most difficult or challenging aspects of their work.

> *Juggling placement work (including the reading you do for placement) and academic work. There are times where there are deadlines close together and sometimes with the best will in the world it is not always possible to work as far in advance as you would like.*
>
> (Year 1 trainee)

> *The most challenging aspects are the academic/research work, although this was generally not as bad as I thought it would be. Also, the length of placements mean that you often feel it is time to leave just as you are getting into it. Be prepared to come out of your comfort zone many times, and become comfortable with uncertainty.*
>
> (Year 3 trainee)

What next?

So far in this book we have aimed to cover the topics, questions and issues that we are most often asked about by people considering clinical psychology as a career. By describing the requirements and processes of getting onto training, what training entails and what the job of being a clinical psychologist is all about, we hope that we have given you information that you will find helpful in deciding whether it might be the career for you. If, after everything you have read from the people who have offered their views and advice, you still feel that you are well suited to the profession, we hope we have given you some useful ideas about how to progress. We strongly believe that the more diverse the profession becomes the better it will serve our society, so do not feel that in order to consider the profession you have to conform to particular stereotypes in terms of race, gender, sexuality, class and ethnicity. The wider the range of experience and diversity we bring to the profession the better.

The next chapter describes what it is like to be a qualified clinical psychologist and some of the many career pathways available over the course of a working life as a clinical psychologist. The final section of the book gives you some ideas about other places that you can seek advice and useful resources.

Starting out as a qualified clinical psychologist and career possibilities

So far in this book we have described what a clinical psychologist is (and isn't). In Chapter 2 we gave you a flavour of what life is like for clinical psychologists working with a variety of people in different settings. We have also talked about the personal attributes, educational requirements and work experience required to apply for clinical psychology training; the process of application and selection; and what clinical psychology training involves.

This final chapter begins by describing what it is like to start a career as a qualified clinical psychologist. We talk about some of the practicalities, what is positive about life post-qualification and what the challenges are. We then go on to outline a number of career pathways for clinical psychologists in order to illustrate the range and variety of working lives that are possible within the profession. This includes the choice of clinical specialties (also see Chapter 2) and of employment settings and employers, as well as possibilities within research and teaching and career opportunities outside of the UK.

What is it like to be newly qualified?

Practicalities

Approximately 95% of clinical psychologists work in the NHS. In Chapter 2 we described a range of NHS job roles and settings. We also discussed other workplaces and roles, such as working for a charity, in education or in private practice. Many clinical psychologists work Monday to Friday 9 am to 5 pm, but this does vary according to service need and roles. Some clinical psychologists are part of on-call systems and some may work evenings and weekends. Within the NHS, the terms and conditions of employment are determined by the Agenda for Change framework. Newly qualified clinical psychologists most commonly start on Band 7. You can find up to date salaries associated with the different grades on the NHS employers website* (www.nhsemployers.org).

Newly qualified Clinical Psychologist – Band 7 (£33,222 to £43,041)
Senior and Consultant Clinical Psychologists – Bands 8a–d (£42,414 to £85,333)

Generally speaking, although there is some regional variation, most newly qualified clinical psychologists secure a job that they want and go straight into their first qualified post. Although there is competition for some posts, the NHS commissions the number of training places according to need so newly qualified clinical psychologists are rarely unemployed.

You will be able to see from the "day in the life of" accounts in Chapter 2, and the reflections of qualified clinical psychologists later in this chapter, that there are many opportunities for career progression and development – sometimes by staying within the same organisation and sometimes by changing jobs. Clinical psychology training equips newly qualified staff to apply for work in any clinical specialty. However, in the more competitive fields, having undertaken a specialist placement and/or research in that specialty may be seen as an advantage by the employer.

What are the positives and challenges of the transition from being a trainee to being a qualified clinical psychologist?

Starting out as a clinical psychologist is exciting and daunting, possibly in equal measure. We interviewed people for this book at different stages of their career; some had only been working as a qualified clinical psychologist for a year or so, others were mid or late career. Everyone we spoke to had accounts to share about starting their qualified career and we noted a number of common themes emerging from their stories.

Imposter syndrome: It is very common for trainees and newly qualified clinical psychologists to doubt their ability to do the job well and to have a sense of not being sufficiently adequate to do the job – to feel as if they are an imposter. Many people continue to feel this to some degree throughout their working lives. Imposter syndrome is an extremely common experience, not unique to clinical psychology and usually well within normal limits. In fact, it can help us to do our job better – being aware of what we do not know and being open to learning is important. To be experiencing some degree of uncertainty and sense that one could/should be doing better is often indicative of an ability to reflect on one's own performance and desire to do the job well. However, the need to be confident and competent when not feeling it does have downsides and during the early stages of a career can be overwhelming. Often related to this is a worry about having to ask for help. This is described by LI, now a very experienced clinical psychologist, who reflects back on the early days of her career:

> *I do remember feeling quite out of my depth and being desperate for reassurance and praise but also feeling that it was totally pathetic to need it and certainly being unable to ask directly for it. I was much more compliant in those days and afraid of doing the wrong thing.*
>
> (LI)

A recently qualified clinical psychologist reflects on his imposter syndrome and sees this as a healthy part of transition:

> *Being qualified came with a healthy dose of 'imposter syndrome' which rears its head from time to time. Losing the student status allows you to step into the shoes of the professional role which at times can feel a little too big. Nevertheless, having your views and opinions taken more seriously by those around you is of great benefit to the people you work with; qualification gives you more weight in helping to promote positive change. The work is draining yet incredibly satisfying, you are constantly learning from everybody you meet and there are always*

opportunities to get more immersed in continued professional development. I wouldn't have it any other way.

(KE)

This is also echoed by DM:

Some years on I still feel like I'm an imposter pretending to know what I'm doing. I still feel like I have to prove myself as a clinical psychologist even after training.

(DM)

In at the deep end: On becoming newly qualified, it is common to feel the impact of working much more independently and not having the high levels of support and supervision that are a central feature of training. This can lead some people to feel anxious and unsupported whilst others relish the sense of independence. However, it is a requirement of our professional body that we have continued clinical supervision, and many other forms of support, such as peer supervision and ongoing learning, should also be available.

Many of the people we spoke to noted the importance of having good clinical and managerial support when they began work.

I feel the biggest challenge that I faced was becoming fully responsible for my own practice and the provision of a service, in contrast to being a trainee when the focus often felt more individualised, led by supervisors and protected from the pressure of service demands. Having the support of experienced clinical psychologists who supported me to develop my skills and confidence was crucial to make this transition.

(SN)

I went into a split post between adult primary care and older adult work. There was no one else working with older people in the mental health services for the area so I felt I was making it up as I went along. I was quiet to begin with and spent quite some time listening. I think this was helpful in terms of not being seen to impose myself but I think I could have been more vocal quicker.

(HC)

Workload level was often noted as a significant change from being a trainee.

I thought it would be easier to be qualified than be a trainee because there seemed like there would be fewer plates to keep spinning, but actually it was just as hard, if not more so, just different.

(KN)

It's hard not to burn out when you qualify – in my experience, the NHS is all about numbers and getting though waiting lists as quickly as possible.

(KM)

Some of the changes were positive though:

It was just so great to have my evenings and weekends back and not to be worrying about writing a thesis – I just had to go to work Monday to Friday like normal people do!

(OK)

Speed of transition: It is common to feel a sense of very rapid transition when starting out as a newly qualified clinical psychologist, which can be disconcerting and unsettling. Only one day separates being a trainee and being qualified and, of course, it takes much more time than that to adjust.

I remember feeling that I couldn't believe anyone would let me practice independently on the Monday after I had still been a trainee and deemed to require close clinical supervision on the Friday before.

(KN)

The training programmes work with trainees approaching qualification to be prepared and anticipate the experience of transition and to consider what support will be helpful. Many services that employ newly qualified clinical psychologists are very conscious of the experience of transition and will provide support and supervision. However, for many clinicians the transition to qualified status remains one of the most significant processes in their working lives.

I can still clearly remember how it felt to start in my first job – the mix of anxiety and pride, feeling out of my depth but also that I was ready to stop being a trainee.

(OK)

Having been through training changes you – a bit like therapy – you can't "un-know" things once you know them. Once you have learned to formulate distress you do it all the time with everyone – yourself and your family and friends. You can't switch off thinking like a psychologist – it affects all your relationships. As you become more experienced your knowledge shifts and becomes more deep-rooted, and you can choose to switch off and what to attend to, but it's very exposing at the start.

(KM)

Continuing to develop skills: Although clinical psychologists are trained to a high level academically, we all continue to learn and to develop our skills throughout our careers. This can feel enormously satisfying and it is a privilege to be in work that continues to build and stretch us intellectually. The jobs we do tend to change and allow opportunities for us to be challenged and develop our practice accordingly.

Since being qualified for five years, I am still enjoying my role very much. Things have changed since I qualified and there are more demands in the role of clinical psychologist which has been tricky at times. I work in a specialist Deaf service in the community and have been involved in some innovative work developing services.

(TQ)

My experience of being newly qualified was very positive. I was fortunate to work in a clinical health psychology department within the NHS and I feel the support of my colleagues was key to a positive and successful transition from a trainee to a qualified clinical psychologist. I was given good advice to focus on continuing to develop my clinical skills, which became my focus over the first two years. . . . As I gained confidence my colleagues were then able to support and encourage me to take on new challenges, such as service development and supervising others.

(SN)

Enjoying the job: Everyone we talked to discussed the aspects of their work as a clinical psychologist that they enjoyed and these were very varied:

> *I really value being an ally for other oppressed groups – I'm a working class gay guy who doesn't fit the usual stereotypes of clinical psychology. I always wanted to help the people who struggle with the stuff I did when I was a kid.*
>
> (KM)

A recently qualified clinical psychologist reflects on aspects he enjoys in his work; how it feels to bring about change and on the variety of the job: "*When the smallest of things change, it quite often feels like a victory. The work is also varied so I'm constantly kept on my toes and generally it's not boring*" (DM).

> *It's fantastic to be in a world where you can learn theory and understand such complex things and understand things that seem un-understandable. You get paid to do it and you can make such a difference to so many people.*
>
> (KM)

> *Ultimately I discovered there's no golden ticket at the end of training and it is just a job, but ever so occasionally I get to feel like I've helped somebody, which is rewarding and perhaps gives me just enough energy to keep having those same conversations.*
>
> (DM)

Career pathways

There are lots of possible career pathways for clinical psychologists. One of the many advantages of the role is the wide range of options of who we work with as well as the types of service setting and ways of working – the "day in the life of" accounts in Chapter 2 will already have given you a good idea of the different sorts of work that clinical psychologists do. For a great many clinical psychologists, the jobs they started when they first qualified have changed markedly over the years, sometimes through circumstances as society and services change and sometimes because they have chosen to make changes themselves. We are often struck by how varied the careers of clinical psychology colleagues are and we are including some of these accounts to demonstrate that the career path does not stop once someone is qualified.

We asked colleagues about their career choices, about what determined the career paths they are on and what advice they would give to those considering clinical psychology as a career.

You will notice a number of recurring themes in these accounts:

Stability or change – whereas some people chose to stay in very similar jobs throughout their careers, others make many very significant changes for a range of reasons.

Choice – sometimes career changes occur because someone decides to do something new, at other times change is imposed by wider factors outside a person's control.

Balancing a career with the other parts of life – many people make career changes to fit with other changes in their life circumstances.

Serendipity – for some people, career change occurs when they are faced with a new opportunity, a chance encounter or a new development.

Variety of employers and systems – you will notice how many people describe working in different systems at the same time (e.g. working in the NHS and a university, working in private practice and the NHS, working for a charity and a public sector employer). Their accounts give a flavour of what is possible, although many clinical psychologists choose to work in one service sector throughout their entire career.

SN (recently qualified – NHS post and now works for a charity)

What is your current job context and type of organisation?

I currently work for a charity which provides emotional, social and practical support to people affected by cancer (i.e. patients and their friends/family). Although we work closely with our colleagues within local hospitals, we are separate from the NHS and provide support to anyone who comes to one of our centres.

What do you do in your current job?

My clinical role within the centre is to provide psychological support through individual and group work. I also supervise and support my non-psychologist colleagues to provide psychological support, both informally and through supervision groups. As the only psychologist, I am responsible for ensuring that the centre works in a psychologically informed way. I also have a regional role as a supervisor of other psychologists and as one of the professional leads for clinical psychology within the organisation.

Why did you decide to do this job and how did you get here?

My main motivation to work for the cancer charity was the opportunity to provide psychological support in an organisation that was dedicated to doing this. I saw the charity as an attractive place to work as it fitted with my own values. Unfortunately, I often felt compromised as a psychologist within the NHS, sometimes by processes, procedures, culture or even physical resources. It was not an easy decision to leave the NHS as I believe it is a remarkable organisation that I feel personally and professionally indebted to. I was also cautious of leaving the safety of the NHS and how working outside it might impact on my career in the long – term. However, I feel that the charity offered me an environment that allows me to practice as optimally as possible; it is a decision I am glad I made.

What are the positives and challenges of your pathway to date and current role?

The positives of my current role are the opportunities that it has given me. I have found working for a smaller organisation with a narrower remit allows for greater flexibility in how I practice and a willingness to try things in different ways. This allows us to adapt to people's needs quickly. Working for a smaller organisation gives me greater opportunity to influence how the organisation operates, which can be challenging, but very rewarding.

The challenges of my role reflect this greater flexibility. Working outside of NHS means moving away from an environment that has clearly defined policies and procedures. Working for a smaller and younger organisation that values a greater level of flexibility means that I need to be able to negotiate dilemmas without defined policies and therefore have a clear understanding of professional guidelines and evidence. It therefore sometimes feels that I have a greater level of responsibility outside of the NHS.

QN (qualified 13 years – works in an NHS primary care service)

Since qualifying I have worked with adults across the age range who are referred by their GPs for a wide variety of psychological difficulties. I've done this job ever since I qualified, but it has changed a lot in that time. When I first started I spent almost all of my time seeing patients in their GP practice. I saw on average six patients per day and really enjoyed the diversity of the community I worked in. After two years, I offered a placement to a trainee and have carried on supervising trainees ever since. To begin with I felt a bit nervous about supervising a trainee and a little self-conscious. However, it helped me to realise how much I do know and this has increased my confidence. I also really enjoy taking trainees because they are enthusiastic, curious and enquiring. As I have become more senior, I now supervise junior qualified clinical psychologists and run a supervision group for them. I have maintained close links with the programme I trained on by providing some lectures and taking on a role providing pastoral support and advice to trainees on the course.

I have kept my clinical skills updated and also learned new therapeutic approaches by attending training courses and conferences. I try to keep up to date by reading books and journals but this is a constant challenge! One of the non-clinical roles that I have developed is as a staff side union representative which means that I represent the interests and employment rights of staff within the organisation. This allows me to feel like I can have an impact that goes beyond delivering individual therapy. I feel really committed to my job and plan to stay.

KM (qualified for nine years – worked in range of NHS services, and is now employed by a university and as a private practitioner)

When I was kid I wanted to be a vet so started doing sciences but then when I was 16 I met a trainee clinical psychologist and knew that was what I wanted to do. I thought that learning to understand other people would help me understand myself. After university I worked as an assistant psychologist in a medium secure service for Deaf people and then in an adolescent inpatient unit.

When I qualified, I wanted to work in adult psychotherapy – I'd experienced psychoanalytic psychotherapy myself before and during training so wanted to continue that but I also enjoyed working with kids. Initially I worked in a Child and Adolescent Mental Health (CAMHS) service full time but had always wanted to be involved in training so later changed to working half time with children with developmental delay and half time at a University. I now work two days a week on a clinical psychology training programme as a lecturer and the rest of the week as private practitioner providing clinical psychology to adults, supervising NHS staff and working with third sector services for children and families around issues of fostering and adoption.

Why did you make the career changes you have made?

I've never been very ambitious in the NHS – I've moved jobs a lot and moved locations too. As I've progressed I do less individual casework but focus on the training and supervision of others.

Why do you do what you do? What's important to you in your work?

Basically I'm interested in how to help the most distressed people – I've worked a lot with issues of suicide and self-harm. I'm interested in oppression and have always chosen to work with people who I feel don't get a fair chance.

Working in training means I get a chance to influence the next generation of clinical psychologists and as a gay psychologist from a working class background I feel a responsibility to be present – and to be seen.

HC (NHS consultant clinical psychologist and professional lead with national roles)

What is your current job context and type of organisation?

I am the lead psychologist for a large mental health and community Trust that employs psychological professionals across all specialties. On a day-to-day basis this means that I'm a point of contact for all of our psychological therapy staff and am responsible for providing senior leadership on psychosocial issues throughout the organisation. As part of my professional lead role, I've developed systems to manage clinical supervision for all clinical staff, making sure that this takes place. I've also developed a framework to review the delivery of psychological therapies within the Trust to ensure that they meet the standards required. I work one day a week in a specialist post-traumatic stress service but spend much of my time presenting the psychological viewpoint to senior staff and supporting colleagues to ensure we maintain professional standards and a reasonable staffing structure despite the pressures of money. I've also been fortunate to be able to be involved with both regional and national work.

Why did you decide to do this job and how did you get here?

My first job post-qualification was a split post working in the NHS in an adult mental health/primary care services for part of the week and the rest of the week working with older adults. I did that job for three years. I worked on older adult wards, started developing out-patient focused work with older people including doing home visits and seeing people in clinic. I always wanted to do more research, so I applied for a post in another NHS organisation which involved doing a needs analysis to develop a primary care service for older people. The job was initially for two years but was subsequently made permanent to enable me to develop and lead the service. I employed counsellors and clinical psychologists to work with me, and had input from occupational therapists and community psychiatric nurses. I also did a PhD part-time whilst I was in this post. I stayed in this job for ten years. After I had finished doing the PhD, I was keen to move on from my post. I think I got this job based on my experience in working for the Commission for Health Improvement (clinical governance really helps with professional leadership), experience in running a small service and also my research experience in doing the PhD. The journey wasn't planned – I've tended to look at things and think that looks interesting I'd like to learn more and that's taken me down different routes.

What are the positives and challenges of your pathway to date and current role(s)?

The positives have been the wide range of opportunities I've had and the different pieces of work I've been able to do. One of the biggest positives/achievements has been successfully completing my PhD. I was fortunate to get funding to do this part-time as well as being able to incorporate some of it into the work I was doing at the time. The challenges relate to my professional leadership role – people don't always understand or value a role which is intended to maintain standards and promote development. Also, promoting a psychological viewpoint in relation to clinical services is not always positively received.

There is still a tendency to defer to the medical model and that can be frustrating.

HL (long career as a consultant clinical psychologist in the NHS and in training/teaching/academic roles)

I qualified as a clinical psychologist in 1986. My first post was in the NHS and was split between working in an adult mental health service and community drug misuse. After three years I changed jobs and worked in HIV and sexual health and I ran a large nationally funded training service. My post was split between providing training, coordinating the training unit and doing related clinical work. The funding ended after some years so I continued working clinically split between physical health specialities. After several years, I took a senior academic tutor post for a university clinical psychology programme and retained two days of NHS clinical work. I now work full time for a clinical psychology training programme and am based in a university, but my post still includes one session a week for direct clinical work.

I have almost always done split posts – whether split between different NHS clinical specialities or split with training posts. For most of my career I have been involved in teaching and training other professionals or professionals in training. My clinical work definitely benefits from my teaching and training roles and vice versa. I enjoy the variety of the work and the challenge of thinking about how to deliver teaching in a way that best suits the audience. I feel incredibly lucky to have been able to do this for most of my career.

There have been some disadvantages to the career path I have taken. Having two different jobs in two different organisations in different geographical areas for many years was logistically difficult. Working two busy part-time jobs meant that I ended up working many extra hours and felt like I did not have enough time in either and I had to focus on the "must dos" of the jobs rather than get involved in the more developmental and exciting aspects of the jobs. I have been qualified 32 years now. I still really enjoy being a clinical psychologist and find aspects to my job all the time that are new and challenging.

LT (worked in the NHS then set up a private business)

What do you do – who do you work for, doing what?

I run a small independent service providing positive behaviour support consultancy and training services to a range of organisations supporting adults with intellectual disabilities, many of whom are also autistic. We provide consultancy around a specific focus person as well as embedding and skilling up services in positive behaviour support through both training and supervision. We also work with a range of specialist schools, supporting the implementation of PBS at a systems level and around specific individuals. I manage the business, the team and also provide a proportion of the clinical work and training sessions.

Why did you decide to do that?

Firstly I would say that I never actually planned to do what I do today – it developed organically. I initially decided to leave the NHS because I felt that I would be able to have a greater impact for the people I worked with by working independently, without the constraints of a large organisation and its systems. However, I am extremely happy with the role that I have now. I have always had a strong interest in working at a systems, rather than an individual, level. This is especially relevant working with autistic adults and children or those with intellectual disabilities where many of the issues experienced by the person are associated with the behaviour of others in terms of the support provided. There are often complex dynamics within a family or a staff team as well as within a wider organisation. Being able to provide interventions that are not based on an individual referral but about getting the right approaches in place across an organisation is what I enjoy most about my role and the work we do as an organisation.

Being my own boss is a major advantage for me; I have the ability to decide what I do and when and where to take the business next but there is the downside that I have all the responsibility and sometimes no one to truly share it with.

Any advice for those considering clinical psychology as a career?

Don't assume that you know exactly what you want to do. Clinical psychology training provides a great range of experience and you might discover an interest or talent that you weren't aware you had. I would always advise working within the NHS for a number of years, firstly to recognise that your training has been funded by statutory services and secondly the clinical governance systems (quality assurance of clinical services) within the NHS are of a high standard and provide an essential ethical and value base to your work.

Clinical psychologists working outside the UK

The ways in which mental health is understood can vary hugely across different cultures within the UK and beyond, and delivery of mental health care can vary significantly from one country to another. Some clinical psychologists who qualify in the UK go on to work in other countries; there are exciting and fulfilling careers and opportunities to make a different type of contribution to alleviating emotional distress and increasing well-being in people's lives. Clinical psychologists contribute to the many global mental health projects around the world (see, for example, White, Jain, Orr & Read, 2017).

Clinical psychology training is very different in other countries so, if you are interested in working outside the UK, it is important to find out more about the specific place where you want to work and the training requirements. You may need to undertake additional supervised practice or exams in order to become registered and licensed to practise abroad. Some of the most common destinations we are aware of clinical psychologists working in include Ireland, Australia, New Zealand, Africa and the Far East.

One of our colleagues went to work as a clinical psychologist in Uganda shortly after she qualified as a clinical psychologist in the UK. She shares her experiences of this here:

> *After graduating and working as a locum clinical psychologist for six months, I got the opportunity to work at Butabika Hospital and live in Kampala, Uganda, for ten months – it was a wonderful experience.*
>
> *Butabika Hospital, the only mental health hospital in the country, has both inpatient and outpatient facilities. It has a total of 500 beds with usual bed occupancy rates of 100%.*
>
> *I had the opportunity to work in a number of areas, including teaching and training, clinical and non-clinical supervision and contributing to service development. I also briefly worked in Rwanda in a consultation role for the Rwanda Allied Health Professions Council as a part of a team setting and reviewing licensing exams for clinical psychology practitioners in the country.*
>
> *A great piece of advice I received when arriving in Uganda was to "be like a fisherman" for the initial weeks, i.e. "to sit, wait and observe". Observing, adjusting and coming to understanding of a new culture, ways of working and unfamiliar systems was an interesting process and I questioned many of the things I thought I "knew". "What does recovery really mean in the context I am working in? How can people be best supported on their journey to recovery in a setting where resources are so limited? What adjustments do I need to make to my approach? How can I be relevant and effective in my work?"*
>
> *I reflected on the realities of many people living in Uganda and their direct link with mental health, including poverty, challenges in accessing education and health care, low employment rate and gender inequalities as well as often having strong community and family support systems. I also wondered about the cultural differences in understanding mental health. After hearing various accounts of service users' experiences with traditional/faith healers, I thought about the impact of cultural beliefs about mental health on self and social stigma and the complexities of introducing other explanatory models for mental health problems and distress.*
>
> *Adjusting to and working effectively within such a different cultural context has been a challenge, and I certainly got it wrong on many occasions. With much more to learn ahead, I feel very fortunate*

> *to be in a profession that offers such variety in areas of interest and specialisation, endless opportunities to learn and develop, work in diverse environments and subsequently make a valuable contribution.*

Throughout this book we have tried to ensure that you have heard a range of voices and opinions of clinical psychologists who have had widely differing experiences of training and working in the field. There are as many views and stories as there are clinical psychologists and this book cannot represent them all. We aimed to give a flavour of what the job entails and can be, and whether it might be the career for you. We hope that we have answered the questions that you have, or have at least indicated where you might find those answers, and that you will have a clearer sense of whether you are the kind of person who might suit the profession of clinical psychology. Whether or not you decide to proceed with pursuing this particular career, we hope that you have found this a useful and interesting book.

Endnotes

* All salary figures are taken from the Agenda for Change salary scales for England from 1st April 2018.

Useful reading and resources

British Psychological Society (2011). *Guidelines for clinical psychology services.* Leicester: British Psychological Society.

The British Psychological Society (2014). *National mental health, well-being and psychological therapies: The role of clinical psychology a briefing paper for NHS commissioners.* Leicester: British Psychological Society.

The British Psychological Society (2018). *Applied practitioner psychologist internship programmes and unpaid voluntary assistant psychologist posts.* Leicester: British Psychological Society.

British Psychological Society, Division of Clinical Psychology (2018). *The Power Threat Meaning Framework: Towards the identification of patterns in emotional distress, unusual experiences and troubled or troubling behaviour, as an alternative to functional psychiatric diagnosis.* Leicester: British Psychological Society.

Davey, G., Lake, N. & Whittington, A. (Eds.) (2015). *Clinical psychology.* 2nd edition. Sussex: Routledge.

Johnstone, L. & Dallos, R. (Eds.) (2013). *Formulation in psychology and psychotherapy: Making sense of people's problems.* 2nd edition. Sussex: Routledge.

Knight, A. (2002). *How to become a clinical psychologist: Getting a foot in the door.* Sussex: Routledge.

Llewelyn, S. & Murphy, D. (Eds.) (2014). *What is clinical psychology?* Oxford: Oxford University Press.

Newnes, C. (2014). *Clinical psychology: A critical examination.* Ross-on-Wye: PCCS Books.

Randall, J. (Ed) (in press). *Surviving Clinical Psychology: Navigating personal, professional & political selves on the journey to qualification.* London: Routledge.

Rhodes, E. (2017) Honest, open, proud. *The Psychologist, 30*, 10.

Shah, S., Wood, N., Nolte, L. & Goodbody, L. (2012). The experience of being a trainee clinical psychologist from a black and minority ethnic group: A qualitative study. *Clinical Psychology Forum, 232*, 32–25.

Turpin, G. & Coleman, G. (2010). Clinical psychology and diversity: Progress and continuing challenges. *Psychology Learning & Teaching, 9(2)*, 17–27.

Weatherhead, S. & Flaherty-Jones, G. (Eds.) (2011). *The pocket guide to therapy: The 'how to' of the core models.* London: Sage Publications Limited.
White, R. G., Jain, S., Orr, D. M. R. & Read, U. (Eds.) (2017). *The Palgrave handbook of sociocultural perspectives on global mental health.* UK: Palgrave Macmillan.

Websites

British Psychological Society's Alternative Handbook. https://shop.bps.org.uk/
British Psychological Society Division of Clinical Psychology Pre-Qualification Group. https://www.bps.org.uk/member-microsites/division-clinical-psychology/dcpgroups
British Psychological Society Jobs. www.jobsinpsychology.co.uk/
British Psychological Society's Minorities in Clinical Training Group. https://www.bps.org.uk/member-microsites/division-clinical-psychology/dcpgroups
Clearing House for Postgraduate Courses in Clinical Psychology. www.leeds.ac.uk/chpccp/
Disability Confident Scheme. www.gov.uk/government/collections/disability-confident-campaign
Health and Care Professions Council. www.hcpc-uk.co.uk/
NHS Agenda for Change Pay Scales. www.nhsemployers.org/your-workforce/pay-and-reward/agenda-for-change/pay-scales/annual
NHS Employers Website. www.nhsemployers.org
NHS Jobs. www.jobs.nhs.uk

Index